THE BACK NINE

By John D. Bowling

PublishAmerica
Baltimore

© 2005 by John D. Bowling.
All rights reserved. No part of this book may be reproduced, stored in a retrieval system or transmitted in any form or by any means without the prior written permission of the publishers, except by a reviewer who may quote brief passages in a review to be printed in a newspaper, magazine or journal.

First printing

Author's note: Some names were either changed or edited out of the manuscript because specific permission to use the name was not granted.

ISBN: 1-4137-4693-4
PUBLISHED BY PUBLISHAMERICA, LLLP
www.publishamerica.com
Baltimore

Printed in the United States of America

Dedication

This book is dedicated to Martha, my wife of forty-eight years, loving mother to our three children, and patient partner in all my endeavors. Whatever I chose to do to earn a livelihood or as a hobby to ward off the boredom of a working man's life, she was always there for me and supportive of my efforts in every way. She ran our home, tended the children, paid the bills, and never complained. When her parents grew too old to care for themselves, we moved them into our home and she became a loving care-giver to them. She was thankful for their long and productive lives. She's a person of immense patience, deep faith, and loving kindness. I'm a lucky man to have her.

Acknowledgments

I extend my sincere thanks to those recreational golfers that have allowed me to use our shared experiences to make this book possible. There are hundreds of other golfers, not mentioned by name in these pages, who inspired me to write about senior golf and the great pleasure it brings to all of us. Sincere thanks also to the membership of the Middle Georgia Senior Golf Association and The Golden Tee Senior Golf Association for allowing me to serve them in a leadership position. I will always strive to deserve their confidence.

I'd be remiss if I didn't acknowledge the staff and management of the golf courses in the middle Georgia area, that have worked with me so diligently to bring the pleasures of golf to seniors in our communities. A special thanks to Tommy, Randy, Lou Ann, and the rest of the staff at Waterford Golf Course for the senior tournaments they sponsor every 2nd and 4th Thursday. Practically every senior I talk with is grateful for their acceptance of us both as patrons and friends.

Special thanks to my grandson, Jessie A. Bowling, who did the cover photography and design. Both of my grandsons, Jessie and Jake, inspired me to write my autobiography as well as this memoir. It all began as a project to leave with them a record of my life that they might appreciate after I'm gone.

Finally, I extend my heartfelt thanks to Danna Tanner, for her immeasurable assistance in proofreading and editing the manuscript.

Table of Contents

Chapter One..09
Introduction
Chapter Two..12
The Front Nine
Chapter Three..19
The Players
Chapter Four...31
The Venues
Chapter Five..34
Making-the-Turn
Chapter Six...40
The Club Surgeon
Chapter Seven...56
Senior Golf Associations
Chapter Eight..61
The Middle Georgia Senior Golf Association
Chapter Nine...66
Other Senior Golf Associations
Chapter Ten...71
Dogfights, Golf Passes, and Scrambles
Chapter Eleven..76
Marshals
Chapter Twelve..91
Overnight Trips
Chapter Thirteen..96
Friendly Bets
Chapter Fourteen...99
Mannerisms and Habits
Chapter Fifteen..103
Special Moments
Chapter Sixteen...115
Starting a Senior Golfers Association.

Chapter One

Introduction

Unlike many sports, golf is played without the supervision of a referee or umpire. The game relies on the integrity of the individual to show consideration and sportsmanship and to abide by the rules. Players should conduct themselves with discipline and demonstrate courtesy and sportsmanship at all times, irrespective of how competitive they may be. This is the spirit of the game of golf.

We all know the great names in golf who have contributed so much to the soul of the game. Think of them. Bobby Jones, maybe the best amateur the game has ever known and architect of Augusta National and The Masters. What about the "Wee Man", Ben Hogan, and his incredible comeback from a life threatening automobile accident? Byron Nelson won eleven consecutive tournaments, a feat that may never be topped. Sam Snead, the sweet swinging West Virginian, won professional tournaments in five consecutive decades. Arnold Palmer, Jack Nicklaus, and Gary Player thrilled us with their competitive zeal in the 1960s and contributed so much to our enjoyment of the game.

Arnold Palmer titled his book *A Golfer's Life*, and it was an interesting read. I can't compare my life to that of a golfer because, comparatively speaking, I'm not much of a golfer. But looking at my golfing experience as the front nine covering my life in golf during my working years, and the back nine covering my golfing life since I retired, might just interest you. Perhaps you'll find some comparisons to your own golfing experience. In the following pages you'll find some descriptions of my golfing experience and meet some of the people with whom I played golf throughout my life. You won't find anything resembling advice on how to play the game, only how to enjoy it on a budget. Because my early golfing life was not at all spectacular or particularly noteworthy, I entitled this book *The Back Nine*. Unlike the pros, I made no breakthrough wins. Unlike the really good amateurs, I never competed for a national amateur title, or for that matter, a local amateur title. I was just an average working stiff who was exposed to golf and learned to love it more and more as the years went by. Therefore, it's not surprising that the most interesting and enjoyable of my golfing experiences occurred in the latter part of my life, especially those years after I retired from the work that earned my livelihood.

Golf, while a frequent and enjoyable pastime during the working years, never occupied the special place then that it became after I retired and could devote more time and energy to the sport. Some of the people with whom I've had a close relationship would tell you that I have a type "A" personality. That's one who demonstrates a take charge kind of attitude when confronted with a problem or objective. This will become more apparent later when you see how I plunged head first into such projects as establishing a golf course, and then a country club in my home town where none had ever existed before. It will be even more evident as I explain my approach to creating a new and challenging hobby after I retired, and how I involved myself in the organization and participation in senior golf in the Middle Georgia area. This book may be the last, or at least the latest, demonstration of this personality trait.

There are literally thousands of people who are finding the sport of golfing an enticing way to get a little exercise, enjoy the fellowship of old friends, and build new friendships after retirement. Many of these are newcomers to the sport. They've either never played the game with any regularity, or they are entirely new to the sport. They have realized that golf is the one physical activity that can be enjoyed as long as they are fairly healthy. Many of them are finding, as I have, that it doesn't have to cost a lot of money to participate in this sport once or twice a week.

In the following pages, I'll give you an idea of my involvement in the game, some of the more interesting people I've met, and with whom I've become good friends. I'll tell you how you can become a member of a senior golfing organization or even start one if none exists in your area. What I will not do is attempt to give you any instruction on how to play the game. If you need instruction you'll need to consult your local professional or a good friend who is willing to give you some free advice. There's plenty of that around. The problem with free advice is that it may be worth what you pay for it.

Golf is played hole by hole. Each hole has an established par. This means that from the time you tee up the ball until you putt it into the cup, par is the number of stokes established as a standard. Most amateurs score well above the standard for an eighteen-hole round. But as the saying goes, "even a blind hog occasionally finds an acorn." That simply means that luck enters into the equation, and even the high scorers sometimes score a par or a birdie. Such instances may cause a novice player to get fired up and spend inordinate amounts of time practicing or going back to the course time after time in an attempt to replicate the feat. There is a broad range of players that score from very close to par, to far above par. In order for the higher scorers to compete with those that shoot close to par there has to be a handicap, and we'll see how some of the senior groups apply this handicap. The eighteen-hole round is divided up into two nines, normally called the front nine and the back nine. Some players have a penchant for the 19th hole, a term applied to the bar in the clubhouse where great shots are relived ad nauseam.

We'll approach this story of my involvement in the game of golf as if it's an eighteen-hole round. I won't bore you with a hole-by-hole account, just a front nine and a back nine.

Chapter Two

The Front Nine

My first exposure to golf came when I was in high school. It wasn't as a player but as a caddie. I thought it might be an easy way to earn a few bucks to spend on the other activities that interested me more. I was wrong on both counts. It was neither easy, nor did it earn enough to support those other activities. There was a golf course between our house and the high school I attended, and I had to walk by it each day on the way to and from school. I noticed some young guys carrying golf bags for the players and made some inquiries about how one might get a job like that. I was surprised to learn that all you needed to do was hang around the clubhouse, look interested, and soon someone would ask if you wanted to caddie. When someone did ask, there was no way to estimate the amount you might earn because it was strictly on a tip basis. If you were lucky enough to catch a golfer of considerable means, you might earn a few dollars for an eighteen hole-round. The downside was that you might catch some poor bloke who could barely afford to pay the greens fees, and in that unhappy event, your earnings would be considerably less. These infrequent caddie jobs had no relation to the caddies who work for the pros you see on television today. Essentially, the caddie of my day was simply a bag carrier. The job of caddie for the ordinary golfer of today has been replaced by the motorized golf cart. During my introduction to the game of golf I don't remember ever actually playing a round. I may have attempted to hit some balls or putt a little, but I never became interested enough to actually play the game. That would come much later in the front nine of my life.

    I was in the Air Force stationed at Goodfellow Air Force Base in San Angelo, Texas, in the mid 1950s when I visited my brother Fred, who was a helicopter pilot stationed at Fort Hood near Kileen, Texas. He had recently been bitten by the golfing bug and invited me to play a round with him and his good friend Charles "Hooker" Amos. My first round was totally forgettable. I'm sure that I had much difficulty making contact with the ball, and I certainly didn't save the scorecard. I must have been less than impressed with the game because I made no immediate attempt to acquire my own clubs and take up the game.

My next memory of playing golf was a few years later, in the late 1950s when I was stationed at Randolph Air Force Base near San Antonio, Texas. We had a base commander who was a golfer and interested in improving the golf course on the base. He was so interested that he asked for volunteers to help clean up the course. I remember that I volunteered to help pick up rocks from the fairways, but I can't remember what the incentive was for the work. Perhaps it was just some time off work, or maybe it was some free golf, or both. At any rate, I became more interested in the game and began to play regularly with some friends from work. One of my bosses, a major, was an excellent golfer and offered to give me a few lessons, which I badly needed and readily accepted. I'm afraid I wasn't a very good student. The one thing I remember him telling me repeatedly was, "You must pronate your wrists." Then he had to tell me what pronate meant. Actually, I couldn't find the word pronate in the dictionary, but I did find pronation. Webster's dictionary defines pronation as "rotation of the hand and forearm so that the palm faces backwards or downwards." I later learned that what he was really trying to get across to me was that during the swing you must roll your hands in such a way that the club face is square to the ball at impact. The reason I was a poor student had nothing to do with my ability. I was a poor student because I didn't devote the time needed for practice. Almost any golfer, from the rank amateur to the touring professional, will tell you that any significant improvement in your game is directly proportionate to the time you spend on the practice range.

During much of my time in the Air Force, I held off-duty jobs to supplement my income. While at Randolph AFB I managed some rental property and as payment for this work I was furnished with a rent free house. The property encompassed nine rental houses situated on 140 acres of land. The houses occupied only a small part of the land and one of the uses I made of the empty space was practicing my short game. My young son at the time was a member of a little league baseball team at the base. We often combined our practice. He would take his baseball glove and position himself at various distances up to 120 yards, and I would use my pitching wedge to hit balls to him. As a result he became very proficient at catching flies, and I became better at hitting greens with a wedge.

We had a fence around our yard, and for a time, I would practice with a sand wedge by hitting balls over the fence. I would place several balls on the grass about two or three yards from the fence, hit down on the ball with my sand wedge, and pop it over the fence. They didn't always go over the fence as I intended, but those that didn't would hit the wire and drop harmlessly to the ground on my side of the fence. I had not considered the risks associated with the base of the fence, which was made of two rows of concrete blocks. Once I sculled a shot, it hit the concrete blocks, bounced back, and hit me in the left temple. It laid me out on the ground and my son went screaming to his mother. When she came to me, I'd just begun to come around. After that I found a safer way to practice with my sand wedge.

My brother Fred was stationed in Germany for three years, and I had little opportunity to play golf with him. Before he came back to the States he bought a new set of Wilson Staff golf clubs, a leather bag, and a Bag Boy golf cart. He had equipped himself for a long association with the game of golf. However, after attending guided missile school at Fort Sill, Oklahoma, he was driving back to his post at Fort Rucker near Dothan, Alabama, and was killed in an accident near Pelahatchie, Mississippi, in October 1959. On my way home to his funeral, we stopped in Pelahatchie, and I viewed the mangled 1957 Ford he had been driving. All of his personal belongings had been removed from the car, but in the open trunk I found some score cards from the Fort Sill Officer and Enlisted Golf and Country Club.

I took the score cards and kept them. He had recently played golf with two guys named Jerry and Herb. He had beaten them quite handily. After Fred's funeral, his wife asked me if I'd like to have his golf equipment. Of course I said I would and took the equipment back to Texas with me. The golf cart had been damaged in the wreck and the 7-iron had a broken shaft. I don't think the shaft was broken in the wreck, but more probably in a fit of temper when a shot went awry. At any rate, I sent the golf cart back to the factory and had it repaired and had a new shaft installed in the 7 iron. I subsequently played many rounds of golf with those clubs while remembering a great brother who had always been my role model. In fact, I played golf with those clubs until the mid to late 1970s when I was a member of Riverside Golf and Country Club in Macon, Georgia. Ray Cutright was the club pro at Riverside. When I asked him about refinishing the Wilson Staff irons, he told me it would cost more than a new set of clubs. However, he did offer me a deal on a much newer set of irons, and I traded the Wilson Staffs to him. He later had the heads re-chromed, new steel shafts put in them, new leather wrap grips put on them, and sold them to one of the lesser known touring pros. He told me who it was, but over the years I've forgotten the name. I did keep the Wilson Staff woods, a driver, 2, 3 and 4 woods. After I retired in 1990 and began a hobby of refinishing and repairing golf clubs, I refinished those Wilson Staffs and retired them to an honored place on the wall of my shop. They are still there, and I never look at them that I don't think of my brother and how much we would have enjoyed playing golf together had he lived.

    One of the great things about golf is the people you meet and the lasting friendships that result from the game. When I returned from Fred's funeral, I began to play more golf. Oscar Newcomb, who was the non-commissioned officer-in-charge (NCOIC) of the machine (Computer) room at work, liked to play golf and so did my friend Hubert "Cotton" Long. We played every chance we got. I remember once playing fifty-four holes in one day when the temperature was 104 degrees, and we walked in those days. When Cotton and Peggy's first child was due, Cotton said, "If the baby comes before midnight, we'll play tomorrow. If it's after midnight we won't." He called me at midnight and said that he had a daughter born at 11:55, so we'll play. And we did. We played many enjoyable rounds of golf at that Randolph Air Force Base golf course where I'd helped to clear the fairways of rocks. In May of 1997, I drove to Heber Springs, Arkansas, to see Cotton. We then drove to Caldwell, Texas, to see Oscar. After driving for almost nine hours, we arrived at about 3:00 p.m. and immediately went to the Copperas Hollow Country Club and played 18 holes. I shot a 76, Cotton had a 77 and Oscar shot an 81. The next morning we went to Randolph Air Force Base and played a round of golf at the course where Cotton and I really began our golfing experience. As Yogi Berra says, "It was deja vu all over again." It had been over thirty years since I'd been on that golf course, and I thoroughly enjoyed playing golf there one more time with two of my favorite people.

We had a great time recalling memorable experiences during our younger days at Randolph. For example, Oscar, Cotton, and I were playing at Randolph Air Force Base in 1961, when I hit a drive off the tee on the fourteenth hole. The tee was elevated and the fairway was bordered on the left by a large man-made lake that extended well over two hundred yards. On the right there was rough of about the same length, but at the end of that rough was a second lake that began just opposite to where the first one ended and continued up the right side all the way to the green. Even though we could hit the ball well over two hundred yards at that time in our lives, it was very risky to try to hit over the lake on the left. Unless we hit it flush in the "sweet spot" we were subject to get wet or end up with a tree in our line on the second shot. If you caught one really well and pushed it or hit a slice, it was possible to go in the water on the right side of the fairway. My tendency back then was to cut or slice the ball, so I could usually count on the ball going from left to right. On this particular occasion I pulled the ball left of the fairway, hit it on a low trajectory, and sent it flying low over the water. We thought for an instant that it might clear the lake on the left. We never saw it splash in the water, so after Oscar and Cotton had hit their shots, we began walking up the fairway. After we'd gone about one hundred yards we saw someone in a black wetsuit wading toward the bank. As we approached we could see that it was a man rubbing his head. When we met him as he staggered out of the water, he said in broken English, "Yell 'fore' the next time you hit in the water." We would have yelled "fore" if we'd seen him, but he was in the water up to his chin searching for golf balls with his feet. He had a burlap bag with him and already had a good number of balls in it. He also had a knot on his head the size of an egg where my ball had struck him. I felt really badly about hitting him, but when the ball hit his head, it bounced to the right and ended up in the fairway. I can't remember what I scored on the hole but this story has been told many times over the years, mostly by Oscar and Cotton.

Another of my favorite memories of Randolph was getting the opportunity to meet my all time favorite professional golfer.

The Randolph Air Force Base golf course hosted a Pro Am tournament in 1961, just before the Texas Open. Arnold Palmer played in the Pro Am, and it was my good fortune to walk the entire 18 holes with him. He talked to me as though he'd known me for years; although that was the first and last time I talked to him. He treated almost everyone that way. I guess that's one reason he's been so popular throughout his career. I had watched him on television just a few weeks earlier at the Masters when he lost by making a double bogey on the last hole. I said to him, "I sweated blood watching you on that last hole at the Masters."

He grinned and said, "I sweated a little myself." On the second hole, he stopped about halfway down the fairway and had his caddie get some band-aids from his bag. I noticed that he had blisters on his hands caused by griping the clubs so tightly. He would stop every four or five holes and change the band-aids. He was in a group directly behind one that included Jack Nicklaus. On the third hole, a par three, he waited not very patiently as Jack lingered for what seemed an eternity over a putt. Finally, he said to no one in particular, "C'mon Jack, hit the putt!"

While waiting on the tee at hole five, a par five, a lady in the small him why he played with such a beat up looking driver. "Wilson furnished you with all the clubs you wanted," she say do," he said, "but when you find a good one, you have to hang to it." This hole was about 550 yards, and we normally played a drive, a lay up, and then a short iron to the green across two streams. There was a lake in the right rough that prevented most of us from taking the short way to the green. Arnold wanted to know how far it was to the far side of the water. We told him it was a 225 yard carry. That was the path he chose, and he played the shot perfectly over the lake. That left him another 250 yards to the green, and he hit a three wood from the rough that came up just short in a trap. He blasted out and two putted for a par.

The fifteenth hole is a par three of 182 yards for the pros. While waiting at the tee for the green to clear, he was walking around talking to people in the crowd. He singled out a little red-headed boy of about five or six and asked him, "What do you think I should hit here?" The boy, not at all shy, said, "A 3 iron." He pulled out his 3 iron and hit the shot pin high on the right, but it ended up in a trap and he took a bogey on the hole. But he sure made a little red-headed boy happy by letting him choose his club.

My barber, whose shop was just outside the base, was a golfer and liked to wager a little. After walking the round with Arnold at the Pro Am, I went to Ernie's barber shop to get my hair cut. While I waited, the conversation turned to golf and the Texas Open scheduled to begin the next day. I told Ernie that I'd take Arnold Palmer against the entire field for the price of a haircut. He jumped at the chance and my next haircut was free. Arnold Palmer won The Texas Open in 1960, 1961, and 1962.

I've only seen Arnold Palmer in person a couple of times since I met him at Randolph Air Force Base in 1961. On each of those occasions it was at a practice round at the Masters, but I didn't get the chance to talk with him.

Chapter Three

The Players

My memorable golfing experiences have been as much about the people I associated with as much as the golf. Whenever I think of a great foursome, the professionals that come to my mind are players like Arnold Palmer, Jack Nicklaus, Gary Player, and Lee Trevino. I suppose the younger generation of golfers is more familiar with Tiger Woods, Ernie Els, Vijay Singh, and Phil Mickleson. The players you meet in these pages aren't even closely comparable to the pros you read about in the papers and see on television. These players are amateurs with no particular fame and chances are you've never heard of them. I'd be willing to bet, however, that if you play recreational golf you will have something in common with most of them. I've already mentioned some of them, but a more detailed introduction might be interesting.

Oscar Newcomb

Like me, Oscar Newcomb began playing golf after he was grown. He first played at age twenty-two while he was stationed in England in the late 1940s. His best round was a 73 and at one time his handicap was down to eight. Oscar is a double retiree in that he retired from the U.S. Air Force as a senior master sergeant in 1966, went to work for civil service, and retired from the Office of Personnel Management as a GM-15 in 1984. We shared a similar career in data processing, now called information management or data automation. Both of us attended college but never graduated. Neither of us played golf in college. Oscar's favorite golfers are Lee Trevino and Arnold Palmer, but he marvels at Tiger Woods and thinks he may be the best to ever tee it up. Oscar has scored a hole-in-one on four different occasions, two of them on the same 130 yard par three, number two hole at Copperas Hollow Country Club in Caldwell, Texas, where he is currently a member. Of more interest is the fact that the two events were separated by thirty-seven years. The first time he was thirty-seven years old and hit a pitching wedge into the hole. The second time he was seventy-five years old and used a six iron. He joined Riverside Country Club when he came to Macon in 1975, and remained a member there until he retired in 1984. After retirement he moved back to Caldwell. However, he has a son who remained in Macon, giving him an excuse to visit a couple of times each year. When he visits Macon, winter or summer, we always play golf and continue to enjoy each others company.

Hubert Long, Jr.

Hubert Long, Jr. began his golfing experience along with me at Randolph AFB in 1958. Back then no one called him Hubert. He was a tall muscular blond, thus the nickname "Cotton." He had a lot of natural athletic ability and played golf as a lefty. He could hit his irons as far as any amateur I've ever known. He retired from the Air Force in 1973 as a senior master sergeant and chief of data automation at Maxwell Air Force Base in Alabama. He then finished his education and settled in Heber Springs, Arkansas, where he became a public school administrator. He holds a B.S. from Troy State University, Troy, Alabama, and master's and specialist degrees from the University of Arkansas at Fayetteville. I understand that he subsequently tried his hand in the retail sales business and became a licensed real estate broker. He was successful in each of his educational and retail ventures and played some golf too. He was a member of the Thunderbird Country Club for eight years and boasts a low round of 67 with a handicap of seven. He later joined the Lost Creek Country Club and has remained a member there since 1996. He has had two holes-in-one, and his most memorable golfing experience was when his playing partner and he had back-to-back eagles on consecutive par four holes. His favorite professional golfer is Jack Nicklaus.

Richard E. Finch

I left Randolph Air Force Base in 1962, having been selected for duty at the air force command post in the Pentagon. I sorely missed my regular trips to the golf course, but the cost of golfing in the Washington, D.C., area was prohibitive for a staff sergeant with a wife and two children. I played golf only once during that assignment. I made friends with a technical sergeant from Mobile, Alabama, by the name of Richard E. Finch. We had some time off during the Christmas holidays and decided we'd try to play a round of golf at the public course on Haines Point. It was a memorable round of golf, not because of the scoring, but because of the conditions in which we played. There was a light snow on the ground, and the golf balls were a little difficult to find, especially if they strayed from the fairway and came to rest in a snow drift. The golf may have been forgettable, but not Richard. We both worked in data processing and frequently used punched cards to produce reports. Punched cards are coded with something called the Hollerith Code. Each card has eighty columns and twelve rows into which holes are punched to represent numbers, letters, or special characters. A zone punch in one of the first three rows, combined with a number from one through nine in the corresponding rows represents alphabetic characters, and occasionally a punch will be dropped and mess up the spelling of a name. Once we produced a printed report in which the zone punch was dropped in the first letter of Richard's last name, thus the report reflected his name as "6inch Richard." From then on he was known by that designation. Who could forget a guy named "6inch Richard?"

Bill Bynum

W. E. (Bill) Bynum is a native of Gadsden, Alabama. His dad worked at the Goodyear Tire and Rubber Company in that city. Goodyear had its own golf course where employees and their immediate families had full membership privileges. Bill began playing golf there when he was eight years old. You might say he cut his golfing teeth on the Goodyear course. He became quite a good golfer and once had a handicap of four. The lowest score he can remember is a 67, five under par. He served in the Navy from 1944 to 1946 as an aviation radio man and was assigned to an air group of PV Ventura twin engine bombers. He played golf only once while in the Navy at a Naval Air Station in Florida. It was a different kind of golf for him because the course had "sand" greens. A rod with a cross piece on the end was used to rake a smooth path to the hole once you reached the green. Bill said three-putting was the order of the day! He attended Auburn University in 1946 and 1947 after leaving the Navy, and subsequently enrolled in the University of Alabama Center in Gadsden from 1948 to 1950. The financial pressures of marriage and a family shortened his formal education to the extent that he never received a degree, and golf was not part of his college curriculum. Bill's favorite professional golfer is Sam Snead, whom he emulates with a smooth, grooved swing. He may not hit the ball as long as Sam, but he is nearly always in play. It's most unusual and a little disappointing, I'm sure, that Bill has never scored a hole-in-one in 69 years of playing golf. Since his talent has failed to produce a hole-in-one, he's now requesting that he be placed on our personal prayer lists. However, Billy Graham, the renowned evangelist said, "The only time my prayers are never answered is on the golf course."

    I met Bill when I was discharged from the Air Force in 1963 and went to work for the Army Missile Command at Redstone Arsenal in Huntsville, Alabama. We worked together in the same section and often shared some of the same assignments as computer systems analysts. We became good friends. I lived in Arab, Alabama, which incidentally, had no golf course. Bill lived in Albertville and was a member of the country club. Some time later, Bill decided to build a new house in Arab and move there. It was a good deal closer to work.

    It wasn't long before we began to explore the possibility of getting a golf course started in Arab. We found a farmer by the name of Melvin Brannon who had a large piece of property close to town.

We felt that it would make a nice nine hole golf course. We approached Mr. Brannon with a proposition. We would form a golf club of at least a hundred people and pay Mr. Brannon annual dues if he would allow us exclusive use of the course on Thursday afternoons and Saturdays. We picked Thursday afternoons because at that time most of the businesses in town closed at noon on Thursday, and Saturday was selected to accommodate those of us who had weekends off from work. We even offered to contact someone who would be willing to design the course for him. He agreed and work began on developing the nine hole golf course that would become known as "Twin Lakes."

The Arab Golf Club was formed, and we kept our end of the verbal bargain we'd made with Mr. Brannon. We contacted a gentleman from Cullman who worked for the state of Alabama and had some experience designing and building golf courses. He came over, laid out the course, and subsequently supervised the construction of the greens. Farmer Brannon knew how to grow grass and the course was ready for play in less than a year. However, we didn't complete our first year of play before trouble arose between the Arab Golf Club and Mr. Brannon. He couldn't resist the opportunity to make a buck. When anyone showed up with green fees, he allowed them to play regardless of the agreement he'd made with our golf club to limit play to club members on Thursday afternoons and Saturdays. The club soon disbanded and reformed later to buy land and build the Arab Country Club.

The Arab Country Club was incorporated in 1965. A board of directors was elected, and we began to sell stock. We bought some acreage on the west side of town and secured a loan from the Farmers Home Administration for $100,000. I was an organizational director and was later elected vice president and served in that capacity throughout the construction phase of the project. Herb Cleveland was president, Bill Bynum was secretary, and Joe Hollis, a local banker, was treasurer. The other board members were: A. C. LaGrone, Tom Mizell, Clayton McGee, Clyde Hart, Billy Joe Treadwell, Vester Thrower, George Gunter, and J.C. Barnard. We built a two-story clubhouse, an Olympic sized swimming pool, two tennis courts, and nine golf holes. Two tees were built for each hole. One set was used for the front nine and the other set was used for the back nine, thus simulating an eighteen-hole course. During the construction phase, I was assigned responsibility for building the swimming pool and was given a budget of $18,000 to spend on it. I had to watch every penny in order to bring it in for that amount. We begged, borrowed, and did everything short of bribing city and county officials for equipment and services to help with the project. This attitude prevailed on all the construction, not just the swimming pool. For example, we used volunteer labor and borrowed equipment to build greens and drainage ditches, clear and plow fairways. And, like most cooperative projects, there were those who worked and there were those who talked. I remember one hot summer day in particular. I was working on the construction of number three green. I had been operating a borrowed tractor grading the green and operating a backhoe constructing the drainage system. I was covered with sweat and dirt when my neighbor, Tom, drove up in his shiny new pickup truck. He was dressed in a suit with tie and began to criticize what we were doing. I stopped and looked him straight in the eye and said, "Tom, what we need is more people to work and fewer people to supervise!" He was bright enough to get my meaning and drove away. I don't remember ever seeing him out there again, even after the work was finished and the club opened for business.

I don't remember what the total budget was for completing the country club, but I believe it was under $200,000 for the land and all improvements. At any rate, it may have set a record for low cost construction of such a facility. It provided many hours of golfing pleasure to a lot of people in Arab and the surrounding area and business at Twin Lakes Golf Course didn't seem to suffer from the competition. Years later, Twin Lakes was sold to new owners, and they expanded it to eighteen holes. It continues to thrive, and as far as I know the country club is doing alright too.

Bill and I were members of the country club for several years. We played together occasionally but were never part of a regular foursome during that part of our golfing lives.

In late 1966 or early 1967, Bill resigned from civil service and went to work for Computer Sciences Corporation (CSC) on a contract to operate NASA's computation laboratory at the Marshall Space Flight Center in Huntsville, Alabama. In early 1967, I also resigned from civil service and went to work for CSC. Bill and I were once again working for the same outfit, but we never worked in the same organizational element. In the mid 1970s, Bill left CSC and went to work for Farrah Clothing Company in El Paso, Texas. In 1976, I also left CSC and moved to Macon, Georgia, to assist another old golfing buddy, Oscar Newcomb, in organizing and staffing a nationwide telecommunications network and computation facility for the U.S. Civil Service Commission. During that same year, Bill called me and wanted to know if he could come to work with us in Macon. He said he either had to move or get a divorce. His wife did not like living in west Texas, and he was willing to accept almost any job to get back to the southeastern United States. He sent me an application, and we were able to get him reinstated in civil service at his old grade. Once again we were working in the same outfit and once again began playing golf together occasionally. We both joined Riverside Country Club in 1976. He continued his membership there long after I gave the game up because of a back injury. During his early years at Riverside, he said he played with some real hustlers who tried hard to separate him from his hard earned money. As familiar as I am with his golf game, I don't think the hustlers were all that successful.

Jorge Buendia

The first time I remember meeting Jorge Buendia was at a senior tournament in Dublin, Georgia, at Riverview Park Golf Course. He played in our group and was also a member of Riverside Country Club. He had been a member of Riverside for years, but I had never met him. I think Bill Bynum knew of him at Riverside, but I don't think they had previously played together. When we first met, Jorge's wife was seriously ill. He always drove his own car and carried his cell phone so that he could be contacted and leave on a moments notice if necessary. Bill and I carpooled to the tournaments and were interested in getting a couple more guys to make up a foursome and take turns driving. From the beginning, Jorge made it clear that he wanted to play in our group, but he also insisted on driving to every tournament. Months later after Jorge's wife died, he still insisted on driving to every tournament. I think part of his reason was that he didn't trust anyone else's driving. Jorge always had two or more cars, but the one he used for golf trips was a 1984 Oldsmobile diesel. We rode many miles in that car and when it finally died, he gave it to his favorite mechanic to use for parts. It had over a half million miles on it!

Jorge has been playing golf for over sixty years. He told me he began his golfing experience in Connecticut during "one of the two weeks of summer." I tried to find out what some of his earlier scores were, but he denied keeping score. It must not have been too bad, however, because he once held a single digit handicap. He was one of the original members of Riverside Country Club. He held membership number 103. In the early days of membership at Riverside, he and a friend, Jack Billman, went in together and bought an electric golf cart. One of his most unforgettable experiences in golf was looking up from a putt one day and seeing his cart rolling down an incline toward a greenside lake with all his clubs and other paraphernalia in it. He and Jack retrieved the cart from the lake, bailed it out, dried off their clubs, and only had to allow one foursome to play through! Jorge doesn't claim a favorite PGA golf professional, he says he likes them all.

Jorge is the only member of our foursome who isn't retired. He owns his own business and claims to be working as hard as he can. He's what I call a "middleman." He represents several manufacturers of restaurant equipment and supplies. He calls on various business establishments and puts together orders for various products such as flatware, serving dishes and cooking utensils. He then arranges for

THE BACK NINE

the products to be manufactured and shipped to the designated business enterprise, and he gets a percentage of the price of the shipment as an agent. He is the sole owner of a corporation known as JABA, Inc. The initials stand for Jorge A. Buendia, and Associates. I never knew who the associates were.

For some time after Bill and I met Jorge, we usually picked up Bill's neighbor and Jorge's friend of long standing, Bill Harrison. Harrison was a little older than the rest of us and was always a little reluctant to play in our group because he didn't score as well as the rest of us. However, we always enjoyed his company. His history was very interesting too. He was a fighter pilot in World War II, and at one time was shot down behind enemy lines in Holland. He hid in haystacks for several days until he could make his way back to American lines. At one time, I tried to get him to let me interview him with the help of a tape recorder, so I could write his story and possibly get it published in a local paper on or around Veteran's Day. I don't know that I could have written the story so that it would have been as entertaining as it was when he told us snippets of it on our way to the golf course, but I would have been willing to give it a shot. Like many other veterans of the great World War, he really didn't want to appear to be bragging about his war time service. So he declined to let me publicize it. Before he retired, he was a traveling jewelry salesman and traveled throughout the southeastern United States. He entertained us with a few of his escapades in that vocation too. Bill Harrison and his wife were both golfers and members of Riverside, but in this case Mrs. Harrison had the reputation as the better golfer.

You might think that driving to a golf tournament from fifty to ninety miles away would be boring. You'd be wrong if you're a member of our traveling foursome. Jorge is a well read individual and holds a business degree from Yale. He has also studied at the University of Havana and the University of Chicago. Immediately after World War II, he was a war crimes investigator stationed in Nuremberg, Germany. There are few subjects on which he cannot converse intelligently. We don't always agree, but he does give forth with an impressive argument. Jorge, being a conservative of the Republican political persuasion, was not a fan of Bill Clinton and his administration, to say the least. If things got boring during one of our trips, all I had to do was make a favorable comment about anything attributed to Bill Clinton or his administration. Then I could just sit back and listen to an opposing opinion for the remainder of the trip!

While a member at Riverside, Jorge continually attempted to get the management to do something to improve the greens and fairways. He even went so far as to take an intensive course in agronomy designed for golf course grounds superintendents. Once he completed the course, he joined a statewide organization of golf course grounds superintendents and attended their meetings. They would meet periodically at different courses, analyze the problems encountered with the course, and recommend solutions based on their collective experience and education. He was even invited to Augusta National and often talks at length about how they keep the Masters' course in such immaculate condition.

Jack Billman and some of his friends organized the Dixie Senior Golf Association in the summer of 1992. Bill Bynum, Jorge Buendia, and I were playing in a Middle Georgia Senior tournament at River North Country Club when we signed up for the new Dixie Association. Jorge had invited one of his long-time friends from Riverside to join our foursome. I had picked up Bill Bynum at his house, and we were on our way to River North. We had just crossed Riverside Drive on Arkwright Road when we saw an old Jeep truck that had obviously died, and the driver was getting his golf clubs out of the back. Bill said, "I'll bet that guy is on his way to River North to play golf." I agreed and decided to back up and offer him a ride. He accepted, and Bill and I met Tom Hartstern for the first time.

Tom Hartstern

Tom Hartstern, a very good golfer at one time, began playing the game in 1945 at the Iroquois Golf Club in Louisville, Kentucky. His first set of clubs had wood shafts. During his prime he was a scratch golfer, that is, he had a zero handicap. His best competitive round was a six under par sixty-six. He holds a B.S. degree in civil engineering from the University of Kentucky and played golf on the university's golf team. Tom entered the Air Force in 1952 and became a general purpose pilot flying both fighter aircraft and multi-engine transports. He served a tour of duty in Korea and once erroneously strayed across the demilitarized zone and was fired on by the North Koreans. Never being one to back off from a confrontation, he fired back at them not considering that he might just start the war all over again. That incident got him into a lot of trouble with his superiors, even to the point where his commission was threatened and his tour in Korea terminated. After returning from Korea, he was assigned to Scott Air Force Base in Illinois. In 1955 he was a member of the base golf team at Scott and often traveled to other bases to compete in Air Force sanctioned tournaments. He left the Air Force in 1957 as a captain and subsequently worked in civil service at Robins Air Force Base in Warner Robins, Georgia, where he retired in 1993. His favorite PGA professional is Bobby Nichols. I guess the fact that he once played a round of golf with Bobby Nichols at Firestone Country Club had something to do with that choice. He describes that round as the highlight of his golfing experience.

Tom joined Riverside Country Club in 1977, where he and Jorge Buendia became good friends. Tom was once a motorcycle enthusiast and bought a new 1987 Susuki 1800 touring model, which he rode across the country from one coast to the other without incident. Two weeks later he was on his way to Riverside on Saturday morning and was hit by a garbage truck, which he said ran a stop sign. He says that was one of eight times during his life that he narrowly averted death. He was seriously injured with many broken bones and there was a question whether or not he would ever play golf again. After a long recuperation period, he was able to take up the game again but not at his previous level of play. He once told me that at one time he had seriously considered turning pro. I assume that was when he was much younger and held that zero handicap. His other close calls included three incidents while flying, two others on motorcycles, and a couple of car/truck accidents.

At one time, Tom lived in Macon. He has been divorced for many years and lives alone. He sold his house in Macon and bought a lot on Lake Sinclair in Hancock County. He put a house trailer on it and took up residence there. We kidded him relentlessly about living out in the sticks, but Tom has a way of just ignoring things he doesn't want to hear. Although he likes to fish, owns a boat, and has built a pier on his property, he plays golf a lot more often than he fishes. Bill and I often urged him to move back to Macon so he wouldn't have so far to travel to play golf with us. It's not unusual for Tom to drive over two hundred miles roundtrip to the golf courses we play.

Tom has two children, a daughter and a son, which he rarely mentions. I'm not sure what the problem is between them, but it's obvious that they don't get along. After we had been friends for several years, Tom was undergoing some medical treatments at Emory University Hospital in Atlanta. During a round of golf one day, he told me that he had listed me as the person to contact in the event of a medical emergency. I don't know what I'd do if I got such a call. I've never been to his home and don't know if I could even find it. One time he had car trouble in Macon, and Bill Bynum drove him home. Bill later told me that Tom lived so far back in the sticks that he didn't think he could find the place again. In a teasing way I asked Tom if he'd also named me as the beneficiary of his life insurance. He just grinned and continued with his game.

Bill, Jorge, Tom, and I became members of the same golf organizations and whenever we played in any of them, we played as a foursome. This association continued for most of the 1990s, 2000, and 2001. Then in 2002, for reasons known only to himself and maybe his wife, Bill Bynum sold his home in Macon and moved back to Arab, Alabama. Once again he's a member of the Arab Country Club.

Chapter Four

The Venues

It's been said that golf is for the wealthy, and for many years that was pretty much the case. You had to be a person of some means to afford to play golf, especially at country clubs. Most fairly large cities have municipal courses, but they are usually less enjoyable venues for play. Municipal courses, while affordable, are usually crowded, especially on weekends. They rarely reserve tee times, so you must show up and get in line. Most of them have a wire ball rack near the first tee. When you arrive, you place one of your golf balls in the rack. Your tee time is governed by when your ball comes out the bottom end of the rack. Frequently, municipal courses are not in the good condition that you find at private clubs, and the reason is simply because of the excessive numbers of players. They literally wear the courses out.

When I moved to Macon, in January of 1976, I was invited to play golf at the city's most exclusive country club as a prospective member. Idle Hour Country Club was indeed a very exclusive club. The initiation fee at that time was $10,000, and after hearing that fact, I didn't ask about the monthly dues. Later I did hear that of the monthly dues, sixty dollars was automatically billed by the restaurant facility, whether or not the member actually ate in or visited the restaurant. In addition to the initiation fee and the monthly dues, assessments were frequently made of the members when major expenditures were needed to maintain, improve, or expand the facility. The golf course remains on rolling terrain with ample wooded areas and a couple of lakes. Some of the most exclusive and expensive residences in Bibb County still surround the course.

One of my good friends, whom I met in one of the senior golf associations, lives just outside the grounds of Idle Hour Country

Club. He is retired from the heating and air conditioning business and often takes his daily exercise by walking along the perimeter of the golf course. He finds an amazing number of quality golf balls, cleans them up, sorts them by brand and puts them in egg cartons. He then gives them away to his friends according to their preference. He has given me several dozens of quality golf balls. They may be used but only slightly. Some of them look like they've only been hit once or twice.

A much less exclusive country club, Riverside, fit my means a lot better, and I became a member there soon after moving to Macon in January 1976. I played there regularly during the remainder of 1976 and 1977 and even won The President's Cup one year. I had a handicap of thirteen, and during the two day tournament I shot a couple of my better rounds, a 76 on the first day and an 81 on the second day. After applying my handicap, the net scores were 63 and 68, thirteen under par.

During those early days at Riverside, I frequently played in a group that included Bill Bynum and Oscar Newcomb. We worked together, and frequently we would take off at noon or a couple of hours early and head for the golf course. I remember one time we had planned to play in the afternoon, and when I left my house to pick Oscar up, it began to rain. By the time I got to his house it was raining so hard that I had to back my truck into his carport in order to load his clubs into the covered bed of my truck. Oscar's wife, Celia, was amazed that we were actually going to the golf course while it was raining so hard. But as is often the case with summer rainstorms, they were scattered, and it wasn't even raining at the golf course when we arrived. We played our round, and when we got home we had a hard time convincing our wives that we had actually been playing golf. On another occasion, we began playing in clear weather, but it began to rain, lightly at first, so we kept playing. I continued to suggest to Oscar that we quit and get in out of the rain. He was reluctant, so we continued and finished the front nine. Again I suggested that we quit and wait for a better day. Oscar was adamant that we continue. He thought it was going to quit raining any minute. We teed off on number ten, played number eleven in the rain and had just arrived at the tee on number twelve when Oscar finally decided that we should quit. By this time, I was already wet so I said, "Hell no! We might as well continue playing. After all, you can only get so wet!" We did continue playing, and when we finished there wasn't a dry thread on my body. I was so wet that even the papers in my wallet were wet. I don't remember Oscar ever being so adamant about playing in the rain again.

Late in 1977 a friend and I were cutting some large pine trees in my yard. After climbing high into one of the trees to attach a rope for guiding the falling tree, I climbed down and swung from a limb and felt the weight of my body pull something in my back. Much later I found that I had herniated disks in my upper spine. I continued to try to play golf but the pain was intolerable. Shortly after the injury, I stopped playing golf, resigned from the country club, and except for an occasional round, I quit playing golf for almost ten years.

When I returned to the game in early 1988, I was preparing to retire and didn't want to invest in another country club membership. I found that I could play as much golf as I wanted without belonging and could play a wider variety of courses. This was a benefit of age and the senior golf association memberships available in the area.

Chapter Five

Making-The-Turn

    The game of golf is one of the oldest participation sports and during the past few decades it's been one of the fastest growing. Have you ever wondered why golf is so popular? I have my own ideas about it. It's a game that you can play alone or with your friends. I always thought it was much more fun for a foursome, but the competition can be against a single opponent or just you against the course. It's a game that gets you outside into the elements and often takes you to some of the more spectacular sights wherever you happen to be when golfing. It's a sport you can enjoy for an entire lifetime. I have friends in our senior golfing organizations that are in their mid to late 80s and still enjoy the game on a regular basis. Some get discouraged because their score goes up in direct proportion to their advance in age, but it beats not playing at all.

    Since I retired, golf has been a great hobby for me. I've enjoyed playing the game. I've enjoyed working on clubs, repairing them, or refinishing them. I've enjoyed the people I've met and worked with in the senior associations, which promote the game simply for the enjoyment of those of us who are retired and still want to be active in sports. I've heard people say, "I tried retirement and didn't like it." Well, I've tried it and I love it. I always have something to do and usually it's something that I want to do and enjoy doing. Very importantly, it's something that I do because I want to, not because I must. I probably know a couple of hundred people in the Middle Georgia area who are interested in playing golf. Some of them belong to two or three different senior golf associations. Most, but not all, of them have relinquished their memberships in local country clubs.

    If this book accomplishes anything, I'd like for it provide an example of what one can do to make golf an enjoyable hobby during their senior years. It can be a guide to other seniors in organizing and operating a senior golf association for the people in their communities who want to enjoy the game well into their senior years. You don't need a lot of money to enjoy golf. I know because I don't have a lot. You might enjoy it more if you have a lot of money and are able to play in places like Hawaii, Hilton Head, or Pebble Beach. But what I'm saying is that you don't need to be wealthy to enjoy the game of golf. I dare say that the guys in my foursome enjoy the game as much as any recreational golfer can. I believe it's not the venue, or the amount of the bets, or the cost of a round that matters most. It's the fellowship we have with one another that makes the game so enjoyable. I would love to travel to Hawaii and play on some of the courses I've seen on television, but if I had to go by myself, or play with strangers, I wouldn't enjoy it nearly as much as I enjoy playing with my friends on courses that are far less pleasing to the eye.

There is one thing about senior golf that does disturb me. That's the tendency of senior golfers to ignore the rules when it's convenient. The traditional view of golf as a sport includes sportsmanship, honor, and integrity. Sadly, in almost all the senior tournaments I can remember playing, I've observed people breaking the rules. One of the most frequent violations is moving the ball or improving the lie. It's pretty much a standard rule in senior tournaments that you can roll your ball in the fairway of the hole you're playing without penalty. There's some justification for this local rule. When you watch a professional tournament, notice the finely manicured fairways. The pros very seldom have a bad lie if they're in the fairway, the exception being if their ball comes to rest in a divot. Even then the divot has probably been repaired by a professional caddie and the lie isn't all that bad. Contrast that with playing on the courses we play, where a lie in the fairway can be as bad as the pros find in the rough. Whether you agree or not, that's the rationale for allowing players to improve their lie in the fairway. This is not completely unknown in the professional ranks either. After a lot of rain you'll note that the professionals are allowed to lift, clean, and place the ball in the fairway. A lot of senior golfers carry this local rule much too far. They improve their lie in the rough, in hazards, or in any other trouble situation in which they find themselves. That is purely and simply cheating, and it really gets under my skin. People who do this don't respect the game, themselves or the people against whom they compete. They may be playing a game that resembles golf, but without complying with the rules or making their own up as they go, they are playing a completely different game. I guess you could say that the average senior golfer is one who starts at six, shouts four, takes five, and puts down three! There are those, however, who think the golf ball should be played as it lies, and I am one of them. We contend that this is part of golf, and if you change the lie you deprive yourself of some of the more fundamental lessons of the game, such as humility and the strength to overcome obstacles in life as well as on the golf course. There is a story about Bobby Jones after he contracted a debilitating disease and could no longer participate in the sport he once enjoyed and dominated. A friend went to visit him and after seeing Bobby's condition, tears came to the visitor's eyes, and he was visibly shaken. Bobby Jones reportedly said to his friend, "Don't feel sorry for me, we must play the ball as it lies."

I don't know many senior golfers who carry a copy of the USGA rules of golf in their bag. I do, and even went so far at one time to order several extra copies that I could give to golfers I observed breaking the rules. It didn't do any good. As they say, it was like whistling in the wind! Many of these guys will agree they're breaking the rules, but will go right on doing so without ever assessing themselves a penalty. Some of them have a hard time keeping up with the number of strokes they make on a hole anyway. I guess they don't want to complicate the arithmetic by adding penalty strokes. George Deukmejian once said, "The difference in golf and government is that in golf you can't improve your lie." Obviously he didn't play golf with the seniors I'm talking about.

While I'm talking about rules, I'll highlight another of my pet peeves. It takes little effort to put an identifying mark on a golf ball. You can color a few dimples in a particular pattern or you can put your initials on the ball. My friend Jorge, having graduated from Yale, marks his ball with several large "Y's" in bright blue ink. No one has difficulty identifying his ball and you don't even have to pick it up to do so. We've been able to identify his ball in several feet of water without retrieving it. Another advantage for Jorge is the fact that when he loses a ball and someone else finds it, they give it back to him. Nobody wants to keep such an ugly ball! Needless to say, all the members of our foursome mark their ball for identification. Some seniors don't want to mark their ball because when they hit it into the woods their chances of finding a ball, any ball, are pretty good. And any ball they find is their ball! Mark Twain once said, "It's good sportsmanship to not pick up lost golf balls while they are still rolling."

The fact that we always have friendly bets insures that members of our foursome abide by the rules because there's always three sets of eyes watching when we play a shot. Just recently, we almost had an altercation in the fairway when Tom Hartstern rolled his ball while in the rough. In Tom's defense, I have to say we were playing in the winter time and the fairway boundary was not easily discernable. Tom claimed he was in the fairway and only admitted his error after the hole had been finished. He won a "rabbit" on the hole, and that made his error even worse. Jorge is like a pitt bull terrier and just wouldn't let it go. He kept verbally jabbing at Tom throughout the remainder of the round. I thought we might be on the brink of a falling out that would jeopardize our foursome. I guess we were saved by the fact that Jorge won the "rabbit" on the back nine.

I enjoy golf too much to dishonor it by violating the rules, and I'm not going to cheat my fellow competitors. I lose respect for those who do cheat. If someone will cheat at golf, what do you think they will do when it comes to the really important things that involve integrity? It's been my good fortune to lead a group of senior golfers we now call the Golden Tee Senior Golf Association. It's operated strictly as an invitational tournament once each month. Each pairing sheet has the more commonly neglected rules printed on the back and the players are always cautioned to abide by the rules. These rules are sometimes referred to derisively as "John's Rules", although they are essentially excerpts from the USGA rules. We had one player who was prone to cheat, not only in tournaments, but every time he played the game. We made it a point to announce before the tournament that we expected the rules of golf to be followed. Bill Bynum and I watched this guy pretty closely because we'd seen him cheat in the dogfights we'd had at Barrington Hall. In a tournament at the Woods in Cochran, Georgia, Bill saw him raking his ball around in the rough and called him on it. After the tournament we checked his score card to see if he'd taken a penalty stroke on the hole. He had not, so we told him he would not be invited to play in our group again. That incident happened several years ago, and he has not played in one of our tournaments since. Everyone who plays golf with this guy sees him cheat, but it's so ingrained in him that he will probably never do any different. Fewer and fewer people will play golf with him. I guess those that still do also disregard the rules. Those that intentionally ignore the rules are not welcome in this particular senior group. I try to be as diplomatic as I can when they complain. I just tell them they might be happier playing their golf in some other group.

    I currently serve as secretary/treasurer of the Middle Georgia Senior Golf Association and was recently able to convince the board of directors to adopt a policy that encouraged players to abide by the rules. During our discussions, someone mentioned that in other senior associations they allow players to improve their lie anywhere. In some they define the fairway as anywhere "from tree line to tree line." I'm sure this travels by word of mouth from one association to another, and it just makes the situation worse. I cannot, in good conscience, condone breaking the rules and urged the board to adopt a policy that explicitly supports the rules. Now, we print some of the more commonly ignored rules on the back of our pairing sheets. We also announce at the beginning of each tournament that we expect everyone to abide by the USGA rules. The rules may continue to be violated by some, but we do not condone such violations. I'm hopeful that this policy will take hold in other associations of senior golfers and that we will begin to see some improvement in this situation. Most people don't want to be known as cheats, so maybe we can shame some of them into obeying the rules.

In the front nine of my life, my expectations about my golf game were much too high. I tried too hard to be like the great golfers I saw on television or read about in the golf magazines. I wanted to hit the ball long and fire approach shots that landed near the pin and spun backwards into or near the hole. Instead, I had a pronounced slice and struggled to exceed two hundred yards on my drives. Too many of my approach shots didn't even hit the green, let alone spinning backward into the hole. I've learned as I've grown older and wiser that you don't have to be good at golf to enjoy it. Jimmy DeMaret, one of the golfing greats, once said, "Golf and sex are the only things you can enjoy without being good at them."

As I approached retirement age, I finally realized that I was never going to be a great golfer. That realization freed me to really enjoy golfing regardless of my score. Don't get me wrong, I still strive mightily to get that birdie or par, to beat my opponent, to win that bet, be it for a quarter or a dollar. I love the opportunity to step on the tee of a beautiful golf hole, breathe the fresh air, feel the warmth of sunshine on my skin, and feast my eyes on the lush, freshly mowed fairways. I love stepping onto a finely manicured green with its subtle undulations and trying to determine how a ball will break as it rolls to the hole. I enjoy it so much that I sometimes putt three or four times on those greens.

"It is almost impossible to remember how tragic a place the world is when one is playing golf." - Robert Lynd

Bill Bynum retired in 1989, and a few months later in the summer of 1990, I retired. We were ready to begin golfing on a regular basis. Bill was a member of the Middle Georgia Senior Golfers Association and put my name on the waiting list for membership. Soon after I became a member of that organization, we were playing in a tournament at River North Country Club and signed up for membership in the newly formed Dixie Senior Golf Association. We were now members of two senior golf groups and became half of a regular foursome for our frequent golf outings.

Harry Vardon said, "Don't play too much golf, two rounds a day is enough."

Chapter Six

The Club Surgeon

A couple of years before I retired, I was discussing the possibility of doing so with my good friend, Carl Bott. He gave me some advice that I appreciated more and more as time went by. He said, "John, when you retire get a hobby or something to do to occupy your time, preferably something where you can earn a few dollars." Carl was a retired electrical engineer and had an impressive shop in his basement. In that shop he repaired television sets. In fact, I met him as a result of an ad in the local newspaper. He had repaired a nice looking Panasonic console television and advertised it in *The Macon Telegraph*. I answered the ad and bought the television. It was such a good deal that I referred all my friends to Carl if they needed a television. He was also a HAM radio operator and was interested in a personal computer to keep track of his friends and contacts. I provided him with a computer and gave him lessons on how to use it.

About two years before I retired, I began building a shop in my backyard. I wanted a place to store my lawn and garden equipment and had ideas of doing some woodworking when I retired. The shop was 16' X 24' with a 10' X 16' shed in the rear. I insulated the walls and ceiling of the main shop so I could air condition it with a window unit. I later designed a propane heater on rollers as a method for heating the shop in winter. Therefore, I could work in comfort regardless of extremes in the weather.

A couple of months before I had my back surgery in August of 1987, we visited my brother, Charles, in Seattle, Washington. Charles was retired and had a well-equipped shop where he did some impressive woodworking. He was also an avid golfer and we played a round at his favorite course while we were there. He provided me with a set of clubs he had refinished, and I was impressed with them. It was that visit and that round of golf that convinced me that I must have something done about my back problem. Consequently, when we returned from Seattle, I contacted a neurosurgeon in Macon and shortly thereafter had a cervical fusion of three vertebrae, which allowed me to play golf once again without pain.

My shop was never completely finished. I began to fill it with tools and tables, and even built cabinets along one wall. As I approached retirement, I made a habit of going to yard sales on Saturday mornings. That's where most of the tools for the shop were purchased. Others I fabricated in the shop. For example, I purchased an old metal lathe at a yard sale and modified it as a sanding machine for refinishing wood golf clubs. The first sanding cylinders were fabricated from the round center pole of an old artificial Christmas tree. I cut the pole in pieces about eighteen inches long, wrapped them with foam rubber, then glued sand paper of various grits to the foam rubber. The sanding cylinders could be inserted into the jaws of the lathe and could be changed quickly. I also covered one of the cylinders with a fine grade of steel wool for smoothing or polishing after the sanding. The cylinder covered with steel wool was ideal for polishing the metal sole plates on wood clubs. I had built an excellent variable-speed sanding machine. The rubber base was perfect for sanding the curves of a wood golf club and I could completely strip a golf club in about five minutes. Another of my homemade tools was a drying box for golf clubs. I bought an old sheet-metal cabinet, modified it with a bottom made of plywood, and cut slots in the bottom so that the shaft of a golf club would fit in the slots. I mounted it at a height where I could hang the clubs so that the heads would remain inside the drying box with the shafts extending through the slots toward the floor. I covered the box with a metal door hinged at the top that would close and keep the warm circulating air on the heads inside the box. The heating element for the drying box was most original. I first attempted to install a heating coil with a thermostat inside the box, but I could never regulate it so that the heat was not too intense. The polyurethane used to refinish wood golf clubs cannot tolerate much heat while curing. The heat has to be gentle and ideally should be circulating around the clubs. Otherwise the polyurethane will bubble up. I finally gave up on the heating coil, and used another of my yard sale items to solve the problem. I had purchased an old electrical heating element from a refrigerator defroster. I fabricated a box, mounted a squirrel cage fan in it, and set it up so that the fan would pull air from outside across the heating element and blow the warmed air through a vacuum cleaner hose to an outlet inside the drying box. The box would dry seven clubs at a time and worked perfectly. I dried hundreds of golf clubs in that drying box and even adapted it with a timer so that it would run the two hours required to dry the clubs and automatically cut off.

When I first began to refinish golf clubs, I didn't want to experiment on very valuable clubs, so once again my yard sale purchases filled the bill. I'd buy old wood clubs, usually for one dollar each and refinish them to look as good as new. When I built up an inventory, I'd take them to the golf course with me and put a "for sale" sign on them. I sold many of them for twenty-five dollars each and the buyers thought they'd found a real bargain. I was following the advice of my old friend, Carl Bott. I had devised a hobby that I thoroughly enjoyed, and it provided enough income to pay my golfing expenses.

My yard sale purchases included many categories of items in addition to tools for the shop or old golf clubs on which to practice my refinishing skills. I once bought a perfectly good Taylor Made Burner driver for just ten dollars. Such clubs sold new in golf shops for around three hundred dollars. That Taylor Made driver is still in my bag and turned out to be one of my favorite clubs. On another occasion, I bought a matched set of four Jack Nicklaus Golden Bear metal woods with graphite shafts for a total of twenty-five dollars. At the same yard sale where I bought the Jack Nicklaus clubs, I also bought a set of four Chicago metal woods with graphite shafts for a total of twenty dollars. These clubs were in excellent condition and needed no repairs or refinishing and as a bonus they came with protective head covers. Since I'd been working on clubs for some time, I knew the value of the club's components. I had bought new graphite shafts exactly like the ones in the set of Chicago clubs to install in newly built clubs, and I knew that I couldn't buy one graphite shaft for what I'd paid for all four clubs. If I decided to cannibalize the clubs and use the shafts in other clubs, I could realize a profit with just one such club.

I've also bought many putters, probably in the neighborhood of twenty, for practically nothing. Some of them were name brand putters like Ping and Zebra. I've never paid over ten dollars for a putter and once bought a collector's item Acusnet Bull's Eye for a dollar. I still have all those putters and change frequently, always hoping that my problems with putting can be cured with a different putter. Of course my friends tell me that "it's not the putter, it's the puttee!"

One of my favorite putters is one I built from scratch. My brother, Charles, who does some amazing things with wood, sent me a small piece of teak and a piece of purple-heart. I fashioned a mallet type putter head out of the teak and used the purple-heart for the putter's face. My friend, Carl Bott, provided me with a piece of brass that provided the needed weight. I inserted the brass into a cutout in the bottom of the teak head and glued the face on to cover the exposed brass on the forward edge. I installed a steel shaft, cut it to length, and installed a putter grip. I finished the teak, purple-heart, and brass in their natural color and coated them with high gloss lacquer. It made a really beautiful putter, the likes of which you cannot buy in a golf shop for under one hundred dollars. I've actually putted with it a few times, and it has a good feel, but it's really too pretty to use regularly. I have promised this putter to my oldest grandson, Jessie, as a memento when I'm gone, although I've never been able to get him interested in golf.

Jessie was born in 1981 and we had some wonderful times in my shop. I cut off some irons and made him a starter set of clubs when he was only five years old. He seemed to enjoy hitting golf balls with me in our yard, and I promised to build him a full set of customized clubs if he would try out for the golf team at school. However, my encouragement wasn't enough to interest him in the game, and his interests turned to art instead.

One time Jessie called and wanted to know if I could build a bridge out of some of the wood I had in the shop. He was five or six years old at the time, and I thought he was talking about a toy roadway bridge. It turned out that he was talking about a bridge like the one on the Starship Enterprise! I told him I didn't know if I could do that because I didn't know what the bridge looked like. He said matter-of-factly, "Well, I'll draw you a picture to go by." The next time he came down from Atlanta, he brought me a picture of the bridge, and I still have that drawing in my shop. With his help we built the bridge using cardboard, balsa, glue, and paint. We even made little chairs from foam packing material into which he could put his Star Trek figures, and we used acetate and pictures from some of his Star Trek magazines to make the display screens on the walls. He was thrilled with the finished product, and I was pretty pleased with it myself.

Another of his favorites at the time was Batman. He asked me to make him a Batman mask to wear to the Halloween party at school. I took him up to the shop, cleaned off one of my tables, and used plaster of Paris to make a mold of his face. He had to lie still on the table for more than thirty minutes while the mixture firmed up. Once I had the face mold, I fashioned a hood using papier-mache and made cardboard cones for the ears. His Batman costume was a big hit at school, and he brought me some snapshots taken at the event. The next Christmas, I built him a bat cave as a present. I spent many hours working on it in the shop. It was made essentially from cardboard and papier-mache. I built tiny little ladders and rails from toothpicks and popcicle sticks that reached from one level of the cave to another. One of the most popular items in the cave was a motorized turntable for the bat car. The motor came from a toy army tank and ran on two flashlight batteries. The turntable itself was a cake tin turned bottom side up. I put a rubber wheel on the motor's shaft and arranged it so that the rubber wheel would roll against the inside of the cake tin making it rotate on a shaft. Of course it was all painted and everything was fitted into a large cardboard box that could be closed for storing. The bat cave was one of his favorite toys, and he kept it for many years.

Jessie was into model building for a period of time and being an avid Star Trek fan, he built many models of the Star Ship Enterprise. He also built some models of the opposing forces. I believe they were called Klingons. We were in the shop one day and he saw me using a soldering iron. He wanted to know if he could use it, and after explaining a few safety precautions, I let him use it to inflict laser damage to some of his models. The scent of the burning plastic was almost too much to endure!

I found many, many toys at yard sales that were in perfect

condition and almost every time Jessie came to visit, which was fairly often, I had new toys for him. Some of those toys we've kept for over fifteen years and now my second grandson is playing with them.

Yard sales continue to be one of the best sources I know for real bargains. I found the key to finding good items was to map out the sales I'd go to on Saturday morning, being careful to limit my stops to the better neighborhoods in town. Some of my other bargains include a Kenwood tuner/amplifier that works perfectly for which I paid just ten dollars. I bought four Sharp speakers for another ten dollars. The speakers worked perfectly with the amplifier, but the fabric that covered the speakers needed replacing. I paid seven dollars for enough new speaker cloth to recover all four speakers and only spent a couple of hours in the shop recovering them. I now have a great sound system with a total investment of twenty-seven dollars, and I've had them in my den for several years and use them daily. I probably couldn't replace the system with a new one for under one thousand dollars.

My friend, Bill Bynum, was continually amazed at the things I purchased for practically nothing at yard sales. He tried it a couple of times without much success. I think you must be handy with tools, have a place to make minor repairs, and go to the sales without any predetermined ideas of specific items to buy. You just happen upon things that you know you can use, either as is or after some minor repairs which you can handle yourself.

I've always enjoyed reading, but after surgery on my right eye I've been unable to read for extended periods of time because of a tearing problem. I discovered audio books as a good substitute for reading. Since my eye surgery I've read, or listened to over three hundred books on tape, and just recently on CDs. Many of the audio books in my private library have come from yard sales at a fraction of the original cost. I also get books on tape from our local library.

One of the venues for our golf was Holiday Hills in Ivey, Georgia. Bill Bynum and I traveled the thirty or so miles up there twice a month to play in their senior scrambles. One of the people I met there and became good friends with, was Herschel Brantley. Herschel and his two sons owned and operated Wilkinson Steel, a steel fabricating enterprise in Wilkinson County, which catered to the kaolin industry. Herschel was a comedic fellow who always had funny stories to tell, and his demeanor totally belied the fact that he was a wealthy man. He prided himself in being a reformed alcoholic and frequently was a featured speaker at AA meetings. He had taken up golf late in his life and didn't pretend to be a skilled golfer. He did enjoy himself on the golf course, however, and kept the group with which he played entertained during the entire round.

Herschel noticed some of the golf clubs I'd refinished and told me he had a set of Jack Nicklaus Golden Bear clubs that he wanted to have redone. I offered to do them for twelve dollars per club and told him if he didn't like them, he'd owe me nothing. When I took them back to him, his comment was, "these are too pretty to hit now!" He said he was going to put them up and just look at them from time to time. He was so impressed with the work that he told another friend, the owner of The Club Doctor in Macon about them.

I knew Louis Etheridge who was the owner of The Club Doctor and had purchased some club heads from him to build the first set of irons that I built from scratch. But after Herschel talked to him, he called me and wanted to talk to me about refinishing some clubs for him. I went to see him and he gave me some woods that were really beat up. He said, "See what you can do with these." I always thought he was testing me with those clubs. I don't think he expected very much so he was totally surprised when I took the refinished clubs back to him. He had a hard time believing they were the same clubs. That began a long association and friendship with Louis Etheridge. When someone brought him a club to repair that was a real challenge, he would call me and have me repair and/or refinish it. Pretty soon I was doing all his refinish work and a good deal of the repair work that included everything from changing the swing weight to replacing the insert or sole plate. One time he had a club for which the sole plate had been lost, and he wanted me to fabricate a new sole plate. I made a paper pattern for it and then cut one out of an old aluminum fan blade. The finished sole plate fit perfectly and was attached with epoxy and brass screws. When the club was then refinished, it looked just like the original except that it didn't have the number and manufacturers name on it. After that, when he needed a sole plate for a club, he'd laugh and tell me he had a club that needed a new fan blade. Other memorable repairs included wood clubs that were split from toe to heel. I'd put them back together with wooden dowels and used epoxy and clamps to make the repairs as strong, or stronger, than the original wood. Again, when they were refinished in black you would never know they were cracked. I used to laugh and tell him, "You may be the club doctor, but I'm the club surgeon."

After we became good friends, I'd go to his store and he'd be too busy to talk to me. It seemed he always had a telephone in his hand. He'd try to work on clubs, operate the cash register, and talk on the phone at the same time. One day I told him I was going to buy him a hands free phone with a headset and microphone. He could attach it to his belt and answer it simply by pushing a button on the receiver/ transmitter. He said, "I wish you would if you can find one." I immediately went to Radio Shack and bought the item, took it to him, and showed him how to operate it. He wore that phone while he was working for several years until he hired additional help, and when he needed something to simplify his busy workplace, he would ask me for recommendations.

At another time, I was in the store when he was searching for a set of steel shafts to install in a set of clubs. He spent much too much time searching through box after box of shafts looking for the right size and flex. Again, I ventured my opinion that what he needed was a set of shaft bins that would hold thirty or forty shafts each, with labels on each bin to identify the manufacture, size, and flex. That way the shafts would stand up vertically and he could store many hundreds of shafts in a lot less space than he was currently using. He then commissioned me to build the shaft bins. I built them in my shop and hauled them down there when they were completed. I also built some work benches for him. He had some rickety tables in the shop that looked like they would fall apart whenever he did any work on them.

I built the work benches out of 2" X 6" pine lumber and made them to fit in the spaces where he needed them. Again, I built them in my shop and hauled them to the store unassembled. I put them together with three inch screws and wood glue. When I installed them, I told him he could stand on them, beat on them with a sledge hammer, or take a nap on them, and they would never waver. Later he had me build some club head racks from floor to ceiling that would hold hundreds of pounds of metal heads arranged so that they were easily accessible. And when it became necessary for him to expand the area of the store, he had me take out some petitions and build counters for displaying merchandise. He paid me whatever I asked for my labor and never tried to haggle over price. It sometimes made me feel that I was working too cheap. What I enjoyed about it was the fact that I was helping a friend, making a little money, and I was my own boss. There were other benefits too. Anything I wanted in the way of golf equipment or supplies, Louis provided to me at his cost. I even bought golf club components necessary to build new sets of clubs for my senior friends and acquaintances. I could build them new clubs, or repair their old ones, much cheaper than they could buy them at retail. My clientele became quite extensive, and I never lacked for top notch golf equipment.

 Louis called me to the store one day to discuss a method to align the spines of golf shafts. He explained to me that golf shafts are rolled and then welded or glued together to attain the tube-like finished product. The lines where the shafts are joined are called spines and are different in density from the rest of the shaft. You can't see the lines when the shafts are finished. When the shafts are installed in the clubs, one club may hit differently from another in the same set because of where the spines are in relation to the club face. The spines also affect the flex of the club's shaft.

 Louis was aware of my homemade tools and wanted to know if I could build a tool that would identify the location of the spine in a shaft. I found that by flexing or bending a shaft and then rolling it you could determine where the shaft was most dense. The effect produced was similar to driving a car with a flat tire. I fabricated a device using pieces of scrap lumber. I first cut a piece of a 2" X 6" about thirty inches long. I then cut two pieces of 2" X 4", one ten inches long and the other fourteen inches. I made cutouts in the 2" X 6" that were twenty inches apart and fit ends of the 2" X 4" into the cutouts. I purchased roller bearings with housings through which I could place a shaft. I carried a shaft with me to Bearings and Drives, Inc. to make sure I was getting the right sizes. I needed two sizes, one to fit the butt of the shaft and one to fit the shaft a little more than half way between the butt and the tip. I then embedded the bearings in the upright pieces of 2" X 4", so that the butt end of the shaft was lower than parallel to the base and the tip end was above parallel. I glued the pieces of 2" X 4" into the cutouts in the 2" X 6" and also glued the bearings into the uprights.

When finished, you could insert a shaft, tip end first, into the larger bearing and run it through the smaller bearing. The bearing on the butt end would stop the movement when it became tight, leaving twelve to fifteen inches of the tip end of the shaft protruding. You could then take a rubber strap or leather belt, drape it over the tip end of the shaft, and with a hand on each end of the strap or belt exert enough tension on the shaft to bend it slightly. With the tension on the shaft, you alternately pull with your hands to roll the shaft in the bearings. As the shaft rolls, you can feel the bump, bump, bump of the spine as it rotates. When the location of the spine is determined, you mark the end of the shaft with a magic marker. When the shaft is then installed in a club, you make sure the mark on the butt of the club is perpendicular to the club face. With all clubs spine aligned, the club builder can insure that a golf ball struck with any club will have the same feel and will fly off the club face the same way. This process may sound simple, but it required several weeks of experimentation to perfect the tool and a few more weeks to learn to use it effectively. I later fabricated a stand for the device and made slots on either side of the stand so that several shafts to be spine-aligned could be stored on one side. After the operator had spine-aligned a shaft he could place it on the other side of the stand until the complete set of shafts were done.

Louis liked to demonstrate his "spine-alignment machine" as he called it, and boasted to his customers that he was the only club builder in the area who spine aligned his clubs.

Another service I provided for my friend, The Club Doctor, was his first computer. I purchased and installed the first computer for the store and acquired accounting and bookkeeping software. I later acted as a tutor for Louis' wife, who did most of the office work, and taught her to operate the computer to input and process accounting and bookkeeping data. We also devised a system for keeping customer information. In addition to the standard data elements such as name, address, and telephone number, we also noted the clubs purchased along with any special items, such as specifications that could be repeated if needed for subsequent orders.

In the fall of 1995, Louis was well on his way to a major expansion. He had rented space in a strip mall located near Eatonton, Georgia in close proximity to the up-scale golf courses located in that area. He was planning to open the new store in time for the Christmas season and had it pretty well stocked with some of his better equipment. Just a few weeks before it was scheduled to open for business, a fire that started in a nearby restaurant, spread to the entire strip mall and destroyed his new store as well as the other businesses there. When the ashes cooled and the fire department and insurance officials had finished their investigation, Louis visited the site and walked through the debris. He picked up a number of club heads, the remains of what had been complete sets of irons on display, put them in a cardboard box, and brought them back to the store in Macon. All the sets of irons he had on display had graphite shafts in them and the fire had melted the shafts and burned all the paint off the heads. Nothing was left but the metal heads, and they were badly discolored from the smoke and heat.

Louis called me to view the remains of the clubs and asked me if I could refinish the iron heads. I looked through them and decided that I could clean them up, buff, or sandblast the stainless steel heads, paint fill the lettering, and make them look almost like new. He gave me the entire box full of heads, and I lugged them back to my shop.

I inventoried the club heads and determined that there were only four or five complete sets of iron heads. I made a deal with Louis. I told him I would clean up the complete sets of irons, and all I wanted for my work was a complete set of the King Cobra heads. He agreed and over the next few months, I'd finish a set of heads and deliver them to him and he would put new shafts in them, new grips on them, and sell them for a pretty good price. It was an especially good deal for him, considering that he'd collected insurance that had covered his cost.

I refinished the King Cobra iron heads and bought new graphite shafts, grips, and ferrules from Louis to build myself a new set of irons. A new set of King Cobra irons at that time sold for over nine hundred dollars so I thought I'd made a pretty good deal. I've been playing with them now for about eight years. They are, by far, the best set of irons I've ever owned.

I still have many of the heads that Louis retrieved from the ashes of that fire. Unfortunately, they are all incomplete sets. Some of the sets only have one or two heads missing. I still have some Pings, First Flight, King Snakes, and one set of Tommy Armour titanium irons. I had to buy some special carbide media to sandblast the titanium heads, which was the only way I could get them cleaned up.

From the early 1990s to the end of the decade, there was a revolution in golf equipment. Metal replaced wood in the long clubs and by the end of the 90s I was refinishing few wood clubs. If I was to continue with my hobby and stay atop of the technology, I had to adapt my refinishing techniques to accommodate the metal clubs.

The first metal clubs I refinished were Taylor Made. They had a bright shiny sole and face, but the body of the club was a metal gray with no discernable paint finish. In order to get the scratches out, I had to sandblast the surface after I had buffed and polished the shiny areas and masked them to protect them from the blasting media.

This process required another shop tool that included an air compressor, a sandblasting hose, nozzle, and a blasting cabinet. I built a blasting cabinet, which was composed of a large box made of plywood. The cover was slanted from back to front, and I inserted a pane of glass in the top so I could view the item being blasted. I had to install a one hundred watt electric light bulb, mounted inside a glass jar, just inside the top cover on the right hand side to provide enough light to clearly see objects being blasted. In the left hand side of the cover I cut a hole big enough to insert the butt end of a club shaft which could include the grip. When the cover was closed, I could hold the shaft end of the club with my left hand while inserting my gloved right hand through a hole in the front of the cabinet to operate the pistol grip sand blasting nozzle. I could rotate the club head with my left hand to apply the blasting force to the area of the club that needed to be sandblasted. The entire cabinet was mounted on a metal stand with wheels so that I could store it in the shed behind the shop and bring it into the shop only when I needed to sandblast a club. The metal stand had a wire basket near the bottom where I could place the container holding the blasting media. A hose was inserted through the bottom of the cabinet and the blasting media was siphoned through that hose by the force of the compressed air going through the blasting nozzle. The used media was collected in the cabinet, and I inserted a tube into the bottom of the cabinet at one end so that I could catch the used media and recycle it after straining it through a screen.

This homemade contraption was used to sandblast hundreds of clubs, including irons. When I'd re-groove irons with a handheld rotary tool, a final step in the process was to sandblast the face of the club and apply a sealer to prevent rust. The irons looked as good as new. Another application for the sandblasting tool included frosting irons. Some golfers wanted their irons, and especially putters, to have a dull finish rather than a shiny one that reflected sunlight. Frosting was done simply by using fine carbide grit to sandblast the entire club. The hardest part of this process was paint-filling the lettering and grooves on the clubs after the sandblasting had removed the original paint. Some club manufacturers began to offer irons with frosted or dull finishes.

New clubs from most manufacturers were now metal instead of wood, and to distinguish one make from another, manufacturers began to paint their clubs. Each manufacturer has its own color. Since I had already refinished some of the earlier Taylor Made metal clubs, the first painted metal clubs I refinished were also Taylor Made. The color was a bronze formulated by PPG Industries exclusively for Taylor Made. I borrowed a new club from The Club Doctor and carried it to a local automobile paint store. I had them mix a base coat paint to match the Taylor Made color and bought a clear-coat to apply over the base coat. The finish produced was exactly like that of an automobile. A hardener was mixed with the clear-coat to keep the surface from scratching easily. I finished quite a few clubs using this technique before I got some complaints about the paint peeling. I consulted my paint store friends, and they suggested an epoxy primer that would make the paint adhere to the surface without peeling. Subsequently, I used the primer on all metal clubs that I refinished.

 It doesn't take a lot of paint to refinish a single golf club, and most of my orders were for a single club. The problem became one of mixing the minimum quantity of paint, primer, and clear-coat to cover one club. I used an air brush, another of my yard sale purchases, for applying the paint. I used a small glass container with a metal lid that I modified to fit the air brush pick-up, and mixed the smallest amount of paint I could. Even then I figured I wasted about half the paint. The paint, primer, and clear-coat each had to be mixed with a thinner, hardener, or catalyst. After the application of each one, the painting equipment had to be thoroughly cleaned with lacquer thinner before going on to the next step. I used pipe cleaners to keep my air brush clean and operating properly. The application of the primer, paint, and clear coat each dried very quickly and the surface of the club was usually ready for the next coat by the time I had the equipment cleaned. Because of the fast drying time, the process of refinishing a metal club was much faster from start to finish than a wooden club, but the costs of materials were much higher.

 In the spring of 2002, Louis went to the doctor for a checkup, and they found a spot on his lung. While he was undergoing tests in preparation for surgery, they also found that he had some serious heart problems. The heart problems were so serious that the surgery on the lung had to be postponed until bypass surgery could be done for his heart. Throughout the remainder of 2002 he was in and out of the hospital several times. When he had recovered sufficiently from the heart surgery, he went to Houston, Texas, for treatment of lung cancer. It appeared that the cancer had gone into remission for a short time, but then it came back worse than ever. This time he did not recover, and in the spring of 2003 he died.

During the time when Louis was ill, I continued to do refinish and repair work for The Club Doctor. I learned, however, that my work had more to do with my friendship with Louis Ethridge than I had imagined. I no longer enjoyed the work, and when it became evident that Louis would not recover, I told Louis that I was retiring again. I did a couple of special repair jobs for him later, but by the time I went to his funeral I had completely abandoned my refinishing and repair work. It had occupied my spare time for over ten years, and while I still do work on my own clubs, my desire to really work at it died with Louis Ethridge.

Chapter Seven

Senior Golf Associations

Senior golf associations are great for those of us who are retired or otherwise can afford to play on weekdays instead of weekends. The associations are usually composed of from one hundred to one hundred and fifty members who are fifty-five years of age or older. They play one tournament each month, usually on a Monday when courses have little play. The courses are willing to negotiate the price per player and the more players you have, the better the negotiating position. Because of the number of players, the association has exclusive use of the course for four or five hours beginning at around nine a.m. Players use a shotgun start so that all the players begin at the same time and hopefully finish at about the same time. Courses can be located anywhere in the commuting area. Some players travel as far as seventy-five or eighty-five miles one-way. Senior organizations also use a modified method of handicapping which serves two purposes, first to speed up play and second to simplify record keeping.

The point system of scoring is similar to the Stableford system and goes something like this. Double bogey gets zero points, a bogey is one point, a par is two points, a birdie is four points, and the rare hole-in-one or eagle is worth eight points. There are no scores over double bogey. When a player lays bogey, he picks up. The Stableford system of scoring was invented in 1931 by Dr. Frank Stableford of the Wallasey & Royal Liverpool Golf Clubs, and the first competition under Stableford rules was played in 1932. The original scoring was as follows: a double bogey is zero points, a bogey is one point, a par is two points, a birdie is three points, an eagle is four, and a double eagle is five points.

Based on the average points a player makes, he establishes his handicap. This allows players of varying degrees of skill to compete with one another. For example, player A may be required to pull twenty-five points while player B is only required to pull ten points. The winner in this case is the one who scores most above his required points. If player B scores fourteen points (plus four) and player A scores twenty-seven points (plus two), player B is the winner, even though he is the golfer of lesser skill. Handicaps work essentially the same way. When a new member joins the group and has an established USGA handicap, his handicap can be readily converted to points. Let's say a new member has an established handicap of fifteen. His points will be set at twenty-one. The calculation is done this way. Under the point system, a player who shoots even par on every hole would accumulate thirty-six points. We simply take his handicap and subtract it from thirty-six to get his starting points. Based on some formula, points are adjusted after each tournament. The formula might be different for each organization, but the principle is the same.

"They say golf is like life, but don't believe them. Golf is more complicated than that." - Gardner Dickinson.

Members usually pay twenty-five dollars for each tournament entered. All members don't play in each tournament but may be required to play in a certain number of tournaments during a calendar year to retain their membership. Sometimes, particularly in the early 1990s, the twenty-five dollar tournament fee included lunch. As the cost of playing continued to rise, some of the organizations dropped the free lunch to avoid raising the entry fee.

An individual may be a member of several senior organizations, and therefore play several times each month at some of the more desirable courses in the area. Following is a typical schedule for one such organization based in Macon:

Typical Schedule

Date	Location
1/12	Houston Lake Country Club, Perry
2/9	Barrington Hall Golf Club, Macon
3/8	Waterford Golf Club, Bonaire
4/12	Riverview Golf Club, Dublin
5/10	Southern Hills Country Club, Hawkinsville
6/14	Healy Point Country Club, Macon
7/12	Pine Bluff Golf Club, Eastman
8/9	Perry Country Club, Perry
9/13	Uchee Trail Golf Club, Cochran
10/11	Little Ocmulgee State Park, McRae
11/8	Oakview Country Club, Macon
12/13	Houston Lake Country Club, Perry

You'll note that one course is scheduled twice during the year. There is no reason to limit the number of times a particular course is played. It all depends on the desirability of playing the course and the price negotiated. Most of the courses will welcome an organization of this type several times each year.

As one who has arranged many tournaments at a variety of venues, I would say that most course officials are eager to have senior groups play at their courses, particularly on weekdays when their amount of play would otherwise be sparse. However, the following example will clearly show that there are exceptions. The Central Georgia Senior Golf Association scheduled a tournament at Oak Haven Golf Course in Macon on November 24, 2003. When we arrived at the course at 8:30 a.m. for a 9:00 a.m. shotgun start it was raining steadily. We waited for almost an hour hoping that the rain would stop and we could play the tournament. At about 9:45 a.m. the president of the association called everyone together and asked if they wanted to play in the rain or cancel the tournament. The group voted unanimously to cancel the tournament and we all went home.

The president, G. C. Andrews, called me the next day and said he had received a call from Mr. Gillis, the owner of Oak Haven, and Mr. Gillis had demanded that the association pay one thousand dollars to Oak Haven because we'd cancelled the tournament. I thought the demand was ridiculous and told G.C. that I wouldn't pay it. Not much was said about the incident for several weeks. Then on January 14, 2004, Mr. Gillis filed a claim against G.C. in the Magistrate Court of Jones County attempting to collect $2098.80 plus $45.00 in costs. His claim stated, "the defendant signed an agreement to pay for a tournament with ninety players at $22.00 per player to include golf, cart fees, and lunch coming to a total of $2098.80. He was acting as the representative of a group called The Central Georgia Senior Golf Association. The defendant asked that the fee be reduced at the time of the tournament and was refused. He and his group then left the premises."

G.C. called me again and was upset that Mr. Gillis was taking him to court. He told me that he had signed an agreement with Oak Haven, but that the agreement specifically stated that there was no guarantee as to the number of players. I asked G.C. to send me a copy of the agreement, which he did. I then had an attorney friend review the agreement, and he also advised that we should not pay the course as requested. He further suggested that the agreement contained no provisions for cancellation and that the inclement weather should be ample cause to cancel a tournament.

We appeared in court on February 12, 2004, and G.C. had some thirty or forty members attend the hearing. Mr. Gillis contended that the tournament was cancelled because he would not reduce the fee from $22.00 per player to $17.50. G.C. had previously tried to get the price reduced because the course advertised a fee of $17.50 per

JOHN D. BOWLING

player during weekdays, which included lunch. However, the price charged had nothing to do with the cancellation of the tournament. In my sworn testimony to the judge, I told him that price had nothing to do with canceling the tournament. I told him that most of our members are elderly and that we didn't play golf in the rain, particularly when it's cold. I also told him that I had arranged many tournaments during the past ten years and that no course had ever attempted to collect when we had to cancel because of inclement weather.

The case was decided in favor of the defendant and we left the courthouse. A few days later G.C. received a letter from Mr. Gillis apologizing for the "misunderstanding" that resulted in the court case. He further offered a free round of golf to every member of the Central Georgia Senior Golf Association. G.C. read Mr. Gillis' letter to the membership at the February 23rd tournament at Hickory Hills in Jackson, Georgia. Not a single member accepted the free round of golf and to a man, said they would never play golf at Oak Haven again. Since then, I have talked to members of several different senior golf associations, and they all said they had played their last tournament at Oak Haven Golf Course.

It's hard for me to understand how a businessman, accustomed to dealing with the public, could make a blunder like this one. If Mr. Gillis had said to G.C., "I'm sorry you had to cancel your tournament because of the bad weather, but if you'll reschedule we'll give you a price of $17.50 per man." I feel sure G.C. would have rescheduled the tournament at Oak Haven and the good will of the course would have remained in tact. Now, because of the law suit, it's doubtful that any other senior golf association will ever schedule another tournament at Oak Haven. It's also evident that a majority of senior golfers in the Middle Georgia area will refrain from playing there as individuals. The law suit was definitely a bad business decision.

Chapter Eight

The Middle Georgia Senior Golf Association

The Middle Georgia Senior Golf Association (MGSGA) is one of the older such associations in the area. It was organized in 1984. The first president's name was Hobbs, but the association was operated by an executive director who was paid by the board of directors to schedule tournaments and negotiate prices for the golf fees as well as for the meals served after each tournament. The executive director was paid with funds collected from the membership for tournament fees and membership dues. The first executive directive and subsequently president for several years was not content with the amount of money he made as executive director and began to sell advertisements in the monthly newsletter that was mailed to each member of the association. He pocketed the funds collected from the advertisements to supplement his income. This arrangement lasted for several years until some of the board members decided they could run the tournaments on a volunteer basis. There was something akin to a revolt among the membership and that executive director moved out of the state. Hubert Moody became president of the MGSGA in 1988 with the board of directors composed of the president, Vice-President Raymond Clark, Secretary/Treasurer Mott Patat and three board members. The MGSGA continued to operate with this group, with some minor changes in officers. For example, the bylaws stated that the president could not succeed himself, so until the bylaws were rewritten and approved by the membership in 1999, the standard practice was to alternate the jobs of president and vice-president at each succeeding election.

The jobs of putting the tournaments together each month and getting the newsletters out were major tasks. Membership records were maintained in a hand written ledger and when each member signed up for a tournament, the member's name and the amount of his check were written in a second ledger. Subsequently, if a member cancelled his tournament entry, his name was scratched out.

Each month, several days before the upcoming tournament, the entire board of directors met, usually at Hubert's house, and prepared pairing sheets by drawing a form on a blank sheet of paper and hand writing the names of each player in a foursome into a block on the form. This process was labor intensive and the margin for error was significant. The finalized pairing sheet was then taken to Office Depot where sufficient copies were made so that each member could pick one up at tournament check-in. After each tournament, the score cards were checked and sorted by score in order to pick the winners. Then the monthly newsletter was produced on a typewriter, copied at Office Depot, and the envelopes stuffed and hand addressed for the then one hundred and fifty members of the association.

Hubert had heard that I was retired from the computer business and asked me to help him adapt the membership records to a newly acquired computer. I readily agreed to do whatever I could to help him and the organization, but soon realized that, as the saying goes, I'd bitten off more than I could chew. I found out rather quickly that Hubert knew absolutely nothing about computers, the software that ran them, or the hardware configuration necessary to do the things he wanted to do. I initially created a data base on my own computer with the essential information on each member of the MGSGA. I then devised a report from the data base that would create an alphabetic list of members. I also created a program to print mailing labels for each member that could be used to send out the monthly mailings. The beauty of a data base is that you can create any number of data fields, sequence reports on any field, and devise reports with only certain selected data fields. You can also filter out data fields that are unnecessary for the task at hand.

My original intention was to develop the system on my computer and copy it to Hubert's and teach him how to use it. I ran into trouble from the beginning. Hubert's computer was a used one he had bought from an individual who was unavailable for any subsequent support. When I attempted to move the system I'd developed from my computer to his, I found there wasn't enough memory on his system to run the program. That's usually not a big problem since memory is fairly cheap and easy to install. But Hubert bought a memory chip that was incompatible with his computer, and when he took it to a computer repair shop for installation, he almost got into a fist fight with the shop owner. I finally convinced Hubert that it would be easier for me to create the documents he needed each month and bring them to him. One thing led to another and I was soon printing tournament documents, printing mailing labels and writing the monthly newsletters. Hubert and I worked in this fashion for several months. The only remuneration for me was that I could play golf in each monthly tournament without paying a fee.

Sadly, Hubert contracted cancer of the liver and died. The vice president at the time was Raymond Clark, who knew I was doing most of the paperwork to support the tournaments each month. He told me he wanted me to continue doing the computer work and eventually used his influence to get me elected secretary/treasurer of the MGSGA. When I took office, I immediately began to review the organization's bylaws. I was appalled that the bylaws had not been updated since the organization's initial charter. It was operated very loosely and minutes of board meetings and membership meetings were nonexistent. Financial reports consisted solely of the bank statements issued by the bank. I took it upon myself to rewrite the bylaws and get them approved by a vote of the membership. I have subsequently been very careful to record accurate minutes of all meetings of the board and membership. Additionally, at each board of directors meeting I provide a comprehensive and detailed financial report.

We currently have a membership numbering one hundred and seventy-five with a waiting list for membership that usually runs between twenty and thirty. Tournament attendance ranges from one hundred on a poor day to one hundred and twenty for the more popular courses. In many cases, attendance is governed by the number of golf carts the particular course can field for the day's play. Members enter tournaments by responding to the monthly newsletter, which includes the tournament course, the price, and the number that can be accommodated. They send in a check for the amount and their payment is recorded in the data base. When the number of applicants reaches the limit that can play, a standby list is maintained and those on standby may get in only if someone has to cancel for one reason or another. Members must play in five or more tournaments in a year in order to maintain their membership. Members may designate a preferred pairing, but if they elect not to designate a pairing, they are paired with players in their general point range. Prizes are awarded in three flights. The first flight is composed of the top one-third of the players arranged by points. The second flight is comprised of the middle third, and the third flight is the third with the lowest points. Each flight therefore competes with players in their own point range. Ten places are paid in each flight and the individual closest to the pin on par three holes is awarded a prize. A special prize is awarded for a hole-in-one during a tournament and is accompanied by a framed certificate commemorating the event. Tournament documents include a pairing sheet that names the four players in each group, the two carts they are to use and the hole-number on which they are to start. The carts are numbered sequentially so they are easy to find. Each player is given a personalized scorecard on which he enters his score and the number of points pulled on each hole. The scorecard contains the player's name and his point quota for the tournament. After the round, the scorecards are collected, checked and the plus or minus score that each player attained is noted on the card. This is how the winners are determined. After that, the scores are entered into the computer data base, a new point quota is calculated for the next tournament, and a new monthly newsletter is created notifying each member of the winners in each flight. The monthly newsletter is also posted to my personal web site along with the annual schedule, rules, and procedures.

 The MGSGA is organized as a nonprofit organization and remains governed by bylaws and a board of directors composed of president, vice-president, secretary/treasurer and three board members at-large. Officers and board members are elected annually by the membership and serve a one-year term. The April tournament each year is designated as the annual membership meeting at which elections are held. Officers and board members take office effective on May 1st. A board of directors meeting is held at least once each calendar quarter, but special meetings may be called by the president or any three members of the board.

Chapter Nine

Other Senior Golf Associations

CENTRAL GEORGIA SENIOR GOLF ASSOCIATION

The Central Georgia Senior Golf Association is very similar to, but different from the MGSGA in that they play their tournaments on the fourth Monday of each month and the CGSGA still provides a meal after most tournaments. However, this is becoming a strain on the finances of the organization and may soon be abandoned. The meal, in most cases, consists of a sandwich or cold cuts with chips and a drink, usually iced tea or water. If the price negotiated with a particular course is such that the organization cannot fund the meal, the members are notified that a meal will not be served. If the organization elects to continue serving meals, an increase in the monthly entry fee may be necessary.

There are also some differences in the way points are adjusted after each tournament. Winners have their points raised by half the difference between their quota and the points scored. For example, if a member has a point quota of twelve points and he scores twenty points and wins, his point quota is raised four points to a total of sixteen for the next tournament. By the same token, if a member fails to score points equal to his quota, his points will be adjusted downward by half the difference between his quota and his actual score.

THE GOLDEN TEE SENIOR GOLF ASSOCIATION

The Golden Tee Senior Golf Association (TGTSGA) began as a loosely organized group of golfers who wanted to take advantage of various pass books such as those offered by the American Cancer Society or the Georgia Professional Golf Association. Other organizations also prepare and solicit sales of their pass books each year, but these two are the ones used by the TGTSGA. In fact, in the beginning this group didn't even have a name. They were sometimes referred to as the Cancer Card Group, or later, the GPGA group.

The TGTSGA is still very loosely organized. There are no bylaws and at this writing no officers or board members. In the beginning, Bill Bynum and I kept the records on members and organized each tournament. Tournaments are scheduled every third Wednesday and members may enter each tournament simply by calling me a day or two before the tournament and telling me they want to play. The only money collected from members for use by the organization is a one-time annual fee of five dollars to offset the administrative costs associated with record keeping and scheduling tournaments. Members pay the fee prescribed by the golf course being played. This usually varies between twelve dollars and twenty dollars per tournament. In addition, an extra five dollars collected from each player at each tournament is used to pay prizes to the winning teams, usually four places.

The point system of scoring is also used in this senior group, but with a little twist. The format of the tournament is alternated each month. One month the tournament is played as a scramble and the next month as individual points. Players are divided into four groups designated as A, B, C, or D players determined by their point quota from highest to lowest respectively. Each team is composed of an A, B, C and D player and the teams are selected in such a way that the total point quota for each team is very nearly the same. The selection of teams is done the same way regardless of whether the tournament is played as a scramble or as individual points. The big difference comes with the scoring.

Only one score is recorded for the team when a tournament is played as a scramble. I should explain for the uninitiated that in a scramble each player hits from the same location. For example, each player hits a drive and the A player, or team captain, selects the best of the four shots. Then each player hits the next shot from that location. The best of the four shots is again selected, and the next shot is played from there by all players. This continues until the ball is holed. The lowest score using the best ball on each shot is recorded. The winners are determined by the lowest medal score recorded for each team. Prizes are awarded by giving forty percent of the prize pool to the first place team, thirty percent to the second place team, twenty percent to the third place team, and ten percent to the fourth place team. Of course the money for each place must be divided among the four team members.

When the tournament is played based on individual points, the score for each individual is recorded. At the end of the round individual scores are totaled and the difference between the teams total point quota and the total points scored will determine the winning teams. Distribution of prize money is the same as in the scramble format.

We have players from time to time who want to change the format, and we listen attentively to their viewpoint. However, we have resisted any substantive changes so far. One such player is Gene Barkley. Gene has a tendency to be very negative and usually has some criticism of just about every facet of the game. He is most critical of his own performance. He can hit a drive fifty yards longer than anyone in his foursome and complains about topping the ball, or hitting it on the toe or heel. It seems that no shot ever comes up to his expectations. Dave Osborn, John Herren, and I were playing in a foursome with Gene at Waterford not long ago when Gene hit a chip shot from the rough. It was his third shot on a par five and it went into the cup for an eagle! Eagles are pretty rare in our group and we were all congratulating Gene on a great shot. Gene's reaction, "it was just a lucky shot, I actually sculled the ball." I've often said to him, "Gene, you've never hit a good shot in your life."

Another of his complaints is the people with whom he is paired. Since everyone is paired based on their point quota, we don't change the pairings just because two players don't necessarily like to play together. In Gene's eyes they either play too slow, or they play so badly they shouldn't even be on the golf course. He often complains about the teams in front of him playing too slowly. To counter this complaint, we let him arrange the teams and starting holes so he could place his team in whatever sequence he felt would most expedite the play. But alas, it seems that Gene just cannot be mollified. Following is an email I received from him recently:

"John, after much soul searching I have come to the conclusion that I do not have the patience to continue playing in the Golden Tee group. I like most everyone in the group, but I get so frustrated on some of the slow play that I have experienced in some of the teams I've been assigned to. I know I'm probably the biggest asshole of anyone that plays in this group, but I have hurt my teams more than helped. It seems I have basically the same people every time. (Francis and Holly). There is no way Francis could pull twelve points."

Gene began playing golf in the mid 1950s while attending Mercer University in Macon. He later served a hitch in the Air Force as an aeromedical technician and reached the rank of airman first class. He was demoted twice for disciplinary reasons but received an honorable discharge as an airman second class at the end of his enlistment. He worked for Nationwide Insurance for eighteen years as an insurance adjuster and sales manager, then for Cotton States Insurance where he retired. He has been a member of Riverside Country Club, River North Country Club, and Barrington Hall Golf Club. He joined Riverside in 1977 and at one time played to a six handicap. He later joined Barrington Hall as a charter member and his handicap shot up to fourteen. He blamed the narrow fairways and Bermuda rough. His most unforgettable experience on the golf course occurred at Sandy Run in Warner Robins, Georgia, when a foursome was hit by lightning during a thunder storm. He and some friends loaded them into their cars and carried them to the emergency room. Two of the players later died from their injuries. Gene now leaves the golf course immediately at the first sound of thunder. His favorite professional golfer is Byron Nelson.

THE DIXIE SENIOR GOLF ASSOCIATION (DSGA)

The DSGA is organized in much the same way as the MGSGA and was established in 1992. It has enjoyed good growth and has recently split into two different monthly tournaments. One is played on the third Monday and the other is played on the fourth Monday of each month. During the past several years the MGSGA and the DSGA have jointly sponsored what is called a Spring Fling and a Fall Fling. These are special outings, usually lasting three or four days and include three rounds of golf. The locations vary, but are always within a day's drive of Macon. In the recent past, venues have included Savannah, Georgia, Saint Augustine, Florida, and Charleston, South Carolina. A joint committee, selected from both organizations, plans the events and negotiates a price for the participants. The price includes the motel/hotel accommodations, three rounds of golf, and one or more meals. Package types include a single golfer, one golfer and a non-golfing spouse, or two golfers. All accommodations are double occupancy. During these special outings, spouses are invited and can play golf in the tournaments if they desire. A separate amount is collected from each golfer to use as prize money for all three tournaments.

There are other senior golf associations in the Middle Georgia area with which I am less familiar. They include the Heart of Georgia Senior Golf Association, usually referred to as the HOGS, the Mid State Senior Golf Association, and the Good Ole Boys Senior Golf Association. All of them have similarities, but their purpose is the same—to make it possible for men to enjoy the game of golf in their so-called golden years.

Chapter Ten

Dogfights, Golf Passes, and Scrambles

Some courses conduct their own senior tournaments, usually called "dogfights", one or more times per month in order to increase their amount of play. One such course on the above schedule, Waterford in Bonaire, Georgia, has a senior dogfight every 2nd and 4th Thursday. This tournament is one of the most popular in the Middle Georgia area. The course is usually in good condition and for thirteen dollars a senior golfer can play eighteen holes of golf, cart included, and if he plays well enough, he can even win merchandise prizes. I'm convinced that the management and staff at Waterford are the best. They always greet their clients with a smile and seem to genuinely appreciate them. About once each calendar quarter, they even treat us to a free lunch of hamburgers and hotdogs grilled especially for us. Without a doubt, the best bargain in golf for Middle Georgia seniors occurs every second and forth Thursday at Waterford Golf Club in Bonaire, Georgia.

More sources of play for seniors, as well as others, are the various golf passes such as the American Cancer Society and the Sectional Professional Golf Associations. These are similar to discount coupons for certain golf courses in a particular geographic area. These golf courses agree to offer discounts to holders of the particular pass, which usually amounts to a few dollars off the going rate for greens fees and/or cart fees. Our foursome, Bill, Jorge, Tom, and I began in the early 1990s to purchase a cancer card each year, both as a contribution to the local chapter of the American Cancer Society and a method of reducing our cost of playing golf at different courses. The first few years we purchased the golf pass, we noted that we used them very infrequently. Subsequently, we began to schedule one tournament each month at one of the courses in the passbook. This way we could be sure to take advantage of the reduced rates. One thing led to another and pretty soon we began to invite other golfers to bring their foursome to our scheduled course, and we could have a little competition among the groups. This method of increasing the number of golfers participating in these monthly events grew at a rapid rate. Pretty soon we had what amounted to another senior golf association conducting a monthly invitational golf tournament on the third Wednesday of each month. This group eventually became known as the Golden Tee Senior Golf Association.

Later we realized that the GPGA golf pass offered a wider variety of courses and in subsequent years ordered the GPGA pass book for everyone choosing to renew each year. The number participating in this group grew rapidly to between fifty and sixty golfers. We also came up with a somewhat unique method of teaming. We ranked the golfers into A, B, C, and D players based on each players average points and one player from each group makes up a team. Competition is based on the total number of points scored by the team, rather than by individuals. The teams that score best against their total points are the winners. This way everyone on the team doesn't necessarily have to score well to win. If one team player scores poorly, another team player may offset that poor score with a good score. When team members enter a tournament, they contribute a small amount to the kitty for prizes, and the top three or four teams win cash prizes. The format is a very popular one and recently we began to play every other tournament in the scramble format.

Those of us who want to play golf more than two or three times a month have ample opportunity to do so. In addition to playing the dogfights at Waterford, mentioned earlier, there are other golf courses that conduct competitive tournaments. Hickory Hills Golf Course in Jackson, Georgia, is one such course. Once or twice each month they conduct a senior scramble. The scramble format is a popular one. Teams are formed by placing A, B, C, and D players in a foursome. Each player drives from the tee, after which the best drive is selected. Each player then hits the next shot from that location. Again, the best shot is selected and the four players hit from that location. This continues for each shot until the ball is holed out. One of the advantages of this format is that when you hit a bad shot, you don't have to play it. I guess that's why it's so popular. These tournaments are a lot of fun and provide great value for the golfing enthusiast. The fee is usually less than twenty dollars, which includes greens fees, golf cart, merchandise prizes from the Pro Shop, and lunch. Considering that most country clubs charge fifteen dollars and up for cart fees in addition to monthly membership dues, you can easily see why these events are such a bargain.

Another venue for frequent scrambles is Holiday Hills Golf Course in Ivey, Georgia. They only charge sixteen dollars per golfer, and one of their drawing cards is a home cooked meal after the round. Prizes and the meal are included in the sixteen dollar fee.

Following is a list of the courses that we play periodically in one senior group or another. Some of them are what we call "up scale" courses. These are the courses around which a housing development has been created and the neighborhoods are very attractive. Some of them are public courses and some are privately owned but are available to the public. Prices for all these courses can be negotiated, usually for less than twenty-five dollars per player, provided they play on a weekday when no other special events are scheduled.

Course	City
Barrington Hall GC	Macon
Bowden	Macon
Brickyard Plantation	Americus
Cottonfields	McDonough
Forsyth CC	Forsyth
Georgia Veteran's State Pk	Cordele
Green Acres GC	Dexter
Griffin City GC	Griffin
Healy Point CC	Macon
Hickory Hills GC	Jackson
Hickory Ridge GC	Thomaston
Highland CC	LaGrange
Highland GC	Conyers
Honey Creek CC	Conyers
Houston Lake CC	Perry
Hunter-Pope GC	Monticello
International City GC	Warner Robins
Lake Spivey GC	Jonesboro
Landings GC	Warner Robins
Links GC	Jonesboro
Little Fishing Creek GC	Milledgeville
Little Ocmulgee GC	McRae
Milledgeville CC	Milledgeville
Morgan Dairy GC	Griffin
Oak Haven GC	Macon
Oakview CC	Macon
Perry CC	Perry
Pine Bluff GC	Eastman
Pine Hills CC	Cordele

THE BACK NINE

Pine Oaks GC	Robins AFB
Raintree GC	Thomaston
River's Edge GC	Fayetteville
Riverside CC	Macon
Riverview GC	Dublin
Southern Hills GC	Hawkinsville
The Cedars GC	Zebulon
The Creek at Hard Labor	Rutledge
The Pines GC	Zebulon
The Woods GC	Cochran
Twin City CC	Sandersville
Uchee Trail GC	Cochran
Waterford GC	Bonaire

Chapter Eleven

Marshals

RIVER NORTH

Soon after I retired, a friend called and asked if I'd like to be a marshal at River North Country Club. I was a little reluctant at first, but conferred with my golfing partner, Bill Bynum, and we jointly decided to check out the offer. The deal was that we would agree to work two or three days per month, either as a starter at the first tee, or a marshal riding around the golf course in a cart looking for problems in the progress of play. Payment for us would be all the free golf we wanted to play at River North on weekdays. We would also have access to the practice range and putting greens at no charge. For a couple of old retired guys who loved to play golf, it sounded like a pretty good deal.

There were sixteen marshals at River North. That might sound like a large number, but remember we only worked twenty-four hours per month—that's three eight-hour shifts. On weekends we had one person who functioned as the starter at the first tee and two people patrolled the course. The starter's job was to insure that tee times were adhered to so that as many golfers as possible could get in a round of golf, especially on weekends. Tee times were scheduled every seven or eight minutes.

Most golfers like to hit a few balls on the practice range to warm up before a round. They also like to hone their putting stroke for a few minutes on the putting green. When they are concentrating on either of these pre-game rituals, they sometimes forget their tee time. It's up to the starter to warn them of their approaching tee time and insure that they get off at the appointed time. If a player fails to arrive for his tee time, the starter has two choices. He can scratch the individual/group or take the next tee time in line and work the tardy group in at a later time. It's highly unusual to scratch a foursome and this is not usually done without the approval of the head golf professional. Remember, these people are all members of the country club, and as a rule, are treated with great deference. One method of resolving this problem is to leave open every 10th or 12th tee time and work the tardy group into one of those slots.

Another problem the starter often faces is that involving the various betting arrangements that groups make before they tee off. Ideally, these arrangements are made before the group gets to the first tee, but practically, they seldom are. Worse yet, is a group of twelve to sixteen golfers who reserve three or four tee times and wait until they get to the first tee to decide who is going to play in each foursome. This situation also complicates the betting arrangements. You can readily understand that a starter on a Saturday or Sunday morning is a pretty busy and sometimes harried fellow.

Marshals patrol the golf course looking for any problems that may impede play. They might also be charged with reminding players to obey certain cart rules, particularly if the course is wet. A golf cart with a couple of one hundred and eighty pound men and another one hundred or so pounds of equipment can make pretty ugly tire tracks on a wet fairway. Some golfers may also forget about the signs at the first tee that proclaim the cart rules for the day. Typically, if play is resumed after a heavy rain, the rule may be "Cart Path Only." This rule actually means that carts are not to leave the cart path at any time during the round. If the course is wet but firm, the rule may say, "Ninety Degrees from Cart Path." This rule means that the cart is to proceed on the cart path until it reaches a point that is approximately ninety degrees from the cart path to the golfer's ball. The cart may leave the cart path at that point, travel across the fairway to the ball and after the shot is played, the cart is supposed to return by the same ninety degree route before advancing toward the green. This is one of the hardest rules for marshals to enforce. You wouldn't believe the varied number of interpretations that players make to this rule. Of course, if no restrictions are in effect, players may drive their cart anywhere on the fairway or adjoining rough, provided they return to the cart path within thirty yards of the green. They should also avoid driving into wooded areas or on any part of the teeing areas.

Normally, one marshal will patrol the front nine holes in reverse order. That is, they begin at the ninth green and traverse the course backwards to eight, seven, etc. The other marshal does the same on the back nine beginning at eighteen. Sometimes, the marshals may change nines periodically to ward off boredom.

The most frequent cause of problems in the progress of play is the group who is extremely slow. When a group is trailing the players in front of them by a complete hole, a problem exists and has to be dealt with before it gets worse. If it isn't resolved quickly, a situation might arise where two or three groups are waiting to tee off on the same hole. This is when tempers flare and members begin to complain to the marshal, the starter, the head golf professional, or the club manager. There are a couple of ways the marshal might resolve such a problem. First, he can politely request the slow group to speed up their pace of play. If two or three such requests fail to get positive results, the marshal may resort to a more drastic solution. He can ask the slow group to hold up and let the waiting group play through. When neither of these actions results in a solution, the marshal may report the slow group to the head golf professional and let him take further punitive action.

While Bill Bynum and I were marshals at River North, we devised a pace chart that determined where any group of golfers should be at any given time based on their tee off time. Marshals could use this chart and a copy of the starter sheet to determine if a group was falling behind in their pace of play. This pace chart was used extensively during the entire time we were employed there.

We worked at River North for three years, through two changes in head golf professionals. From time to time we were aware that some members objected to our working there and getting free golfing privileges. When a new head golf professional was hired that thought we should work an hour for every hour we played golf, the entire staff of marshals quit en masse.

River North Country Club is exclusively private. That is to say you must be a member or a guest of a member to play there. It's one of the better golfing facilities in the Middle Georgia area. The course was designed by Gary Player and offers a challenge for any golfer from the low handicap player to the weekend duffer. The greens are bent grass and very fast. A definite adjustment is required when putting on the greens of other nearby courses. There are four tees for each hole. The gold tees are the longest and are used by pros and low handicap players. The length of the course from the gold tees is 6,644 yards. From the blue tees, the next longest, the course measures around 6,247 yards, and from the white tees, the shortest tees for men, the course is 5,847 yards. Red tees are for women and the length for them is about 5,074 yards. Working at River North as a marshal for three years gave me a new appreciation for golf and all the practice and playing there greatly improved my game. It's no secret that the more you play the game the better you get, that is, until age starts to diminish your physical attributes.

It might be interesting to visualize the course, hole-by-hole.

The following description is from the perspective of a senior golfer hitting from the white tees, since those are the ones with which I'm most familiar. The first hole is a slight dogleg to the right. It measures 365 yards, and from the woods on the right, the rough slopes sharply to the fairway. The terrain levels out across the fairway. There is a shallow drainage ditch in the left rough just at the tree line. A large sand trap is on the left just beyond the bend in the fairway. From the tee, the fairway slopes downward sharply for about one hundred yards, and then slopes gently upward toward the green. Just short of the green there's a sharp incline that makes it difficult to get on the green unless you fly the ball all the way to the green's surface. The green is large and has been carved out of the hill. Sand traps guard the left front of the green and a large grass bunker is on the right. The hole plays to par four and for most amateurs, birdies are rare.

The second hole is a 310 yard par four with a fairway that's narrow for the short hitters, but widens out at around 200 yards off the tee. This fairway is also tree lined left and right. There's a deep ravine on the left that will catch a pulled drive or a hook. The perfect drive is long and if not straight, a slight fade is good. However, a slice may reach an out-of-bounds on the right. The second shot is up hill to a generous sized green. A sand trap guards the right side of the green.

The third hole is a par five 478 yards long. The drive must thread its way down hill between trees on the left and right to a wide and level landing area. If the driver doesn't play a slight draw, it's fairly easy to hit the ball through the fairway. Some of the longer hitters use a fairway wood or long iron off the tee for safety. The second shot, with a fairway wood or long iron, must guard against going left into a large lake that runs all the way to the green. If the ball is played to the right, it goes over a high incline that slopes from right to left until it reaches the narrow fairway. If the ball hangs in the rough of the hillside, it makes for a tricky third shot. Ideally, the second shot stops about one hundred yards from the green on the level fairway. From there, a pitching wedge or sand wedge can reach the green for a putt at a birdie. Water is left of the green and a large sand trap guards the right side of the very large green. For the brave golfer who attempts to reach the green in two, the landing area in front of the green is usually wet, and always soft, providing little or no roll. A good approach shot is rewarded with a good chance for a birdie and an occasional eagle is not impossible.

The fourth hole is a short par three. It's 136 yards up hill to another large green that slopes from right to left and back to front. This green will definitely test your putting skill. One year when the Hogan Tour made a stop at River North, I was a walking scorer and witnessed the following action on the fourth green. One of the pros hit an excellent shot to about eight feet below the pin. He marked his ball while the other players putted. When his turn came to putt, he replaced his ball, picked up his ball marker, and started to putt. When he addressed the ball, it began rolling down the incline. He replaced

THE BACK NINE

it and assessed himself a penalty. Instead of getting the anticipated birdie, he had to settle for a bogey. The difficult putting on this green has resulted in its share of three putts during an otherwise good round.

Number five is a par four of 310 yards downhill. There is trouble both right and left. A slice will almost surely mean a pitchout and a third shot to the green. The left side isn't quite so bad, but woods to the left can mean trouble too. Assuming you keep your drive somewhere in the fairway. The hole plays fairly easy. The second shot usually requires no more than a wedge to the green. However, there is trouble behind the green if you hit it long, and sand traps on the left and right to catch wayward shots. Again, the green is large and slopes from back to front. Par is a good score, but birdie is a definite possibility.

The sixth hole is a 454 yard par five. The tee is elevated and the landing area for the drive is also elevated. There is a small pond in front of the tee, but it's mainly for aesthetic purposes. The fairway is fairly narrow but lies between wooded hills on either side. The rough is cleared of trees for twenty to thirty yards so an errant shot is very likely to take a friendly bounce toward the fairway. The fairway doglegs to the right and the second shot can be made with a fairway wood without fear of going too far. The green is elevated and any approach shot that falls short may roll away from the green. There are sand traps left and right with the green sloping from right to left and back to front. Most of the players I know are happy to two-putt on this green.

Number seven is a long par four of 368 yards mostly up hill after driving from an elevated tee. The fairway is wide once you reach the landing area. However, for those of us who are not long hitters, reaching the landing area is a pretty good shot. The second shot requires a fairway wood or a long iron. The green is flat and very large. It's not unusual to have a putt ranging upward of fifty feet. Sand traps are located on the front left and right. Of the par four holes described thus far, this one requires the best shot making skills. The distance from this green to the next tee makes one appreciate a motorized cart. I mentioned earlier, the Hogan Tour event that was played at River North in the early 1990s. Volunteers with carts at the exits to the greens on number five and number seven would ferry golfers and their caddies from the green to the next hole and the players were most grateful. Not as grateful, however, as the poor caddies carrying those heavy professional bags. The rules provide for no more than fourteen clubs in the bag, but the rules don't limit the amount of other stuff, such as balls, tees, towels, rain gear, food, and drinks that may be contained in the bags. Most of the golfers on this tour don't have full time caddies and several of them had their wives caddie for them. Others employed local caddies.

The eighth hole is my favorite because it was there that I experienced my first of two holes-in-one. The tee is elevated and the green is maybe seventy to eighty feet below the level of the tee. It's 149 yards down the hill, but plays more like 130 yards. Two large sand traps guard the right side of the green and the left side drops off into deep woods. The green slopes from back to front and offers a good test of putting skills when the ball is above or to the side of the hole.

Number nine is another par four that's 340 yards but plays longer. It's flat and straight but is unforgiving if drives stray to the right or left. If the shot goes left and long, the woods cause problems, and if it's short but out of the fairway an uneven lie makes it almost impossible to reach the green with the second shot. It's better, however, than a stray shot to the right where a gaping sand trap awaits the errant shot. If the ball happens to go to the right of the sand trap you're in what we call "jail." The only option at that point is to pitch out and try to make the green in three. The second shot is around 140 yards and the green is fairly level and offers a good possibility of a one-putt. There is a sand trap on the left front of the green. From here we travel past the clubhouse in route to the back nine. The cover of this book provides a view of the 10th hole from the tee.

The entire course is laid out roughly in the shape of a figure eight. From the clubhouse the front nine makes a rough circle left to right and ends up back at the clubhouse. The back nine circles right to left and meanders its way back to the clubhouse. You will note the almost complete absence of water on the front nine. That will change abruptly as we approach the back nine.

The 10th hole is a thing of beauty when viewed from the tee. The fairway slopes down to a large lake that crosses the fairway on a bias from left to right. The shortest distance to the water is on the left. This is not a good place to hit a pull or a draw. The water definitely comes into play. If the ball is played right of center it's possible to hit a full driver. Anything right of the fairway is trouble and will require a lay up before crossing the lake. Assuming you're "straight down the middle," as Bing Crosby says in the song, there is a possibility of making the green in two. However, there is no room for error. The second shot must carry the water but can reach trouble in the woods on the left or bunkers on the right. The green is elevated and is a two-tiered affair. When the pin is set on the bottom-tier, putting from above the hole can be hazardous to your score. I've often thought that the safe way to play this par five hole is to hit three good irons—one short of the lake and in the left center of the fairway, then one across the water to a landing area about 130 yards from the green, and a third to the green. Some of the better hitters would only need a nine iron or wedge on the third shot, but if they're that good, they probably wouldn't want to play that conservatively anyway. The tenth is 446 yards, beautiful to the eye, but strikes terror in the golfer's heart!

The eleventh hole is one of the most unique holes I've ever seen. From the elevated tee, the drive must thread its way through a narrow opening in the trees to a wide landing area. A well-hit draw will reduce the distance to the green on the second shot, provided it is well placed. The second shot must negotiate a fairway that is dissected by a drainage ditch. If the shot is short of the green, it almost surely will wind up in the ditch since the fairway slopes to the ditch on both sides. The green is a large kidney shaped one with severe undulations and a pronounced slope from back to front. There is no sand trap, but why would one be needed? There is plenty of trouble on this 400 yard hole, and most of the golfers I know are proud of a par.

Twelve is another par five that is reachable in two for the big hitters. The fairway bends slightly to the right and a fairway bunker catches anything that attempts to cut the dogleg. The second shot may be attempted with a fairway wood, but if it's slightly long and to the right, there's a drainage ditch along the full length of the green to make those long hitters think twice about going for it. A large and deep sand trap is in front of the green. The green is undulating and not the easiest one to putt. Birdie is a definite possibility on this 436 yard hole.

Thirteen is a par three that plays 138 yards across a lake. There is a bail out area to the right for those who fear the water. Large sand traps guard the green on the right and catch anything that is long. The green is large and slopes from right to left and from back to front. It's a good par three and might yield birdies to those who can hit the green and stay below the pin. One of my most vivid memories of this hole has to do with a round I played while it was raining lightly. My grips were wet and when I swung, the club slipped out of my hand and wound up in the lake with the grip sticking up out of the water. We were able to retrieve the club without wading in and getting even wetter than we already were. I was more careful after that to dry my grips as best as I could before swinging.

Fourteen is a par four 329 yards long. The fairway landing area rises far above the level of the tee with a slight dogleg to the right. The rough on either side of the fairway slopes toward the fairway and tends to funnel errant shots toward the fairway. It's fairly short so the second shot can be made with anything from a seven iron to a wedge, depending on the effectiveness of the drive. The green slopes from left to right and back to front. A large sand trap guards the left front of the green. There's nothing spectacular about the hole and a birdie is a definite possibility.

Fifteen is another par three of 139 yards with a lake along the entire left side from tee to green. Large sand traps in front catch anything that gets over the water but is short of the green. The green is fairly large, but if you're long, there is a steep drop-off that will make par a good score. The green is undulating and not the easiest one to putt, particularly if the pin is on the front.

Sixteen is downhill straight-away 348 yards. A lake comes into play about two hundred yards off the tee so a long iron or fairway wood is the choice from the tee. If the drive is good, you'll have about 140 yards or less to the large flat green. A creek runs along the left rough just across the cart path and will punish a hook or draw. A large trap is in front of the green and the terrain back and right of the green drops away steeply punishing errant shots in that area. The tee shot is the key, and if that's good, a birdie is a possibility but par is usually welcome.

The seventeenth bends ever so slightly from left to right. It's not long but has plenty of trouble, particularly on the right. The fairway slopes from left to right and if the drive lands right of center, it's likely to end up in the right rough with no shot to the green. Most players aim for the steep slope on the left side of the fairway and hope for a good bounce back to the fairway. The second shot must traverse a rock lined creek about twenty yards in front of the green. Just over the creek on the right is a large sand trap. The green is large and slopes from right to left. It's not the easiest green to putt, and a par on this 326 yard hole is sure to bring a smile to the face of the senior amateur.

Eighteen is the signature hole of the course, a par four 370 yards. The drive must either land on an island, or skirt the water by landing in a narrow strip of fairway to the right and short of the water. Avoiding the island shot usually requires a mid to long iron. Some of the longer hitters may want to hit a fairway wood to the island to avoid going through the island and ending up in the water on the other side. The ideal shot lands on the island about 130 yards from the green and makes the hole an easy par. If one elects to lay up to the right, it's very difficult to reach the green in two. In that event, the second shot must carry over two bodies of water and two sand traps before reaching the green. The green slopes steeply from back to front and from left to right. From a position above the hole three putts are not unusual. A view of this hole is on the back cover of this book. If the hole had a name, it would be TROUBLE!

NOTE: River North is still a community in the Macon, Georgia, area, however, the name of the golf course has been changed to Healy Point.

BARRINGTON HALL

I mentioned previously the experience we had being marshals at River North Country Club. After leaving that job, we were satisfied not to be working anywhere. We enjoyed having all our time to do the things we wanted to do. Then one day we got a call from one of the group who had worked with us at River North. He told us that Barrington Hall Golf Club was interested in staffing a marshal program and wanted to know if we'd be interested. We agreed to attend a meeting with the head golf professional at Barrington Hall and make up our minds after hearing the details. The deal was pretty close to what we had at River North in the early days there, with a couple of added benefits. In addition to playing golf without paying cart or greens fees, the club would sponsor a senior dogfight every other week on Tuesday and Thursday mornings. We could invite our friends to play for the cart fee, plus five dollars to go toward the prize pool. We decided this was too good a deal to pass up, so once again we became employee marshals at one of the better clubs in Macon. It was also one of the newest courses and had an excellent layout.

Barrington Hall was built in the early 1990s as an upscale facility with a quality eighteen hole golf course and housing development. It opened in 1992 and at first was advertised as a private club. Initiation fees during the next few years ranged from $900 to $1500 with monthly membership dues of about $115. After the first few years when it struggled to meet expenses, the strictly private aspect of the club was abandoned and the club initiated a "pay and play" policy. It currently operates as a semi-private club with a modest number of memberships, but depends to a large degree on a pay and play clientele.

The layout of the course is excellent but not enough space has been retained between the course and building lots. Consequently, housing has encroached on the course to the extent that golfers sometimes feel they are playing in the back yards of the residents. There is little room between rough and out-of-bounds and on some holes the out-of-bounds are barely off the fairway.

When we began working there as marshals, Roy Jarvis was the head golf professional. Soon thereafter Roy left to become head pro at River North. Bill Bynum and I brought our pace charts that we had developed at River North and implemented them at Barrington Hall. We also developed the program for recording and updating the points for players in the senior dogfights, and a computerized work schedule that insured that weekday and weekend work was applied equally to all the marshals.

While I was working at Barrington Hall, a routine eye exam revealed that I had a recurrence of cancer in my right eyelid. Two years earlier I'd had plastic surgery to remove a tumor in the same place. During that surgery, they removed about a third of my right eyelid and restructured it so that you'd hardly notice after it healed. Because of the recurrence, a technique was used to insure that all cancer cells were removed. This procedure required the entire removal of the bottom lid of my right eye in one operation with a second to reconstruct the eyelid. The reconstruction included a graft of skin from my upper lid to the lower, so my right eye was closed with sutures and had to remain closed for over three months while the graft took. Subsequently, the eye was opened with a scalpel, and after some minor stitching, I had a new bottom eyelid.

I never missed any work because of the eye surgery, nor did I miss any of the senior dogfights at Barrington Hall. But the interesting part of it was trying to learn to hit a golf ball with one eye closed. I found I could hit most shots about as well as I could with two good eyes, but using only one eye just completely destroys depth perception. I found the hardest shot of all to hit with one eye was blasting from a sand trap. During the time my eye was closed, I tried especially hard to avoid sand traps.

Over three years after the eye surgery there appears to be no recurrence of the cancer and the only ill effect is an almost constant tearing that is more a nuisance than anything else. When the bottom lid was removed, the tear ducts that drain the eye fluids into the nasal passages were also removed or grown together. Therefore, there is no place for tears to go, so they spill out of the eye and down the cheek. I consider that a small inconvenience when I think I could have lost sight in the eye. Now, as part of my standard golfing equipment, I carry a good supply of Kleenex, which I refer to as eye mops.

After we had worked at Barrington Hall for about two years, a club member, John Campbell, was appointed as manager of the marshals. Since John had never served as a marshal, he was unfamiliar with the kinds of situations marshals often encounter as evidenced by an incident that occurred during one of the dogfights. John was playing in our foursome that day. One of the cardinal rules marshals attempted to diligently enforce was that of not allowing golf carts within thirty yards of the greens unless they were on the cart path. We were waiting to hit our second shots to the eighth green when we saw a cart on the right side of the green near the putting surface. It should have been on the cart path on the opposite side. Rather than reporting the violation to the marshal on duty or to the pro as would have been proper, John assumed the marshals authority and took it on himself to walk up the fairway and yell at the group on the green, telling them they were in violation of the cart rules. At this point, Hal Beam, one of the players on the green and incidentally a member of the club, met John about twenty yards in front of the green and decked him. In the melee they both fell to the ground. By the time we reached the site of the altercation, John had gotten up and Hal had returned to the green. Even though John was out of line in his assumption of authority, we thought the behavior of Hal Beam was worse and urged John to report the incident at the turn. When we finished the ninth hole, we all went into the pro shop to speak with the pro. The head pro wasn't in so we spoke with his assistant. John reported what had happened, and we told the assistant that we too had witnessed the whole thing. I further expressed the opinion that Hal Beam should be ejected from the course and not be allowed to come back. The assistant got in a cart and proceeded to find Hal as they finished the tenth hole and were leaving the green. After a short discussion between them, we noticed that the assistant got in his cart and returned to the clubhouse. Hal continued with his round. The assistant later explained that he thought it was just a "mutual misunderstanding", and unless John was willing to swear out a warrant for Hal's arrest, nothing further would be done. Even though John may have exceeded his authority, this incident seriously diminished the assistant's standing in the eyes of the marshals. John elected to drop his complaint and nothing more was done about the incident. I'm still bothered by the fact that while John's actions were not altogether proper, the actions of Hal Beam were much more serious. On the one hand John may have been guilty of poor manners, but Hal Beam was guilty of assault!

Some time later, I was working the back nine and noticed a foursome across the number thirteen fairway in their carts. At this particular time, the cart rule was "cart-path-only." I drove over and politely reminded them that they were supposed to be on the cart path. One of the players became hostile and threatened that he would "whip your ass." I noted the cart numbers and left to report the incident to the head golf professional. When I found him playing on the course, I told him about the incident and informed him that "I should not have to put up with such conduct." He agreed and later told me that he had discussed the situation with the individual in question, and that he had told him that any further conduct of that kind would result in his expulsion from the club. There was not another occurrence that I'm aware of, but I thought it would have been appropriate to require an apology at the least. Subsequently, if there was any violation by this group, I just reported it to the pro and considered my job done. It was evident to me that anything short of murder would be tolerated by members as long as they paid their monthly dues. Although there were other incidents, I don't know of anyone who was ever expelled for bad conduct.

As I've stated previously, one of the primary reasons for having marshals is to control the pace of play. Most of the people on a golf course are very nice and cooperative, but occasionally you run into the exception as evidenced by the preceding paragraphs. Once in a while, you'll run across an individual who resents being watched. They are particularly perturbed by marshals watching them from a distance. One day I had very politely advised a group of members that their pace was just a little slow and asked them if they could "please pick it up a little." Then I drove my cart to a spot between the ninth green and the tenth tee and parked it there to observe the pace of the groups making the turn. Butch McCarty, a member who was in the group I'd talked to earlier about their pace, approached the ninth green and drove his cart to where I was parked. He told me to "get the hell away" and quit bothering them. I told him that I was an employee of the club, and that he had no right to tell me where I could park my cart. He became belligerent, spouted off about how he had helped build the course and was a charter member. I told him I didn't see how that affected my job, whereupon he threatened me with bodily harm. I have to tell you that considering my physique as compared to his, this situation was almost funny. Butch is a skinny little guy about 5'8" and weighs about 140 pounds. I tip the scales at about 230 and am about six inches taller. When he threatened me, I just gave him a steady gaze and said, "Be careful now, you don't want to do anything stupid." I didn't move my cart until they were well away from the tenth tee.

We worked at Barrington Hall for about three years and had many great rounds of golf there. Our tenure as employees ended much as it had at River North when a new pro, Keith Brady, was hired and thought the marshal program was not effective. He didn't exactly end the program, but made it impossible for us to continue to work there. For example, he decreed that in the future marshals would be required to pay the same cart fee that members paid. That resulted in my leaving as well as several others. A few stayed on for a period of time, but the marshal program was effectively dead.

We have continued to play there occasionally, sometimes as a foursome and sometimes our senior golf association will book a tournament there. Bill Bynum joined Barrington Hall as a member after the marshal program ended, and I sometimes played in his group on a pay-and-play basis.

Chapter Twelve

Overnight Trips

Venues for our golf outings were not limited to the Senior Golf Associations. Beginning in the mid 1990s we began to participate as a foursome in several different golf outings. Some were sponsored by the Senior Golf Associations and some were not.

The Middle Georgia and Dixie Senior Golf Associations jointly sponsor two outings each year. One is called the Spring Fling and takes place sometime during late March to early May. Another is called the Fall Fling and it takes place in late September to early November. These events are usually three or four days in length and take place at some resort type facility within a day's drive of Macon. Savannah is a more frequent choice, but we have had these events in Myrtle Beach and Charleston, South Carolina, Waynesville Country Club in Waynesville, North Carolina, and St. Augustine and Destin, Florida. A committee of both associations arranges the events and negotiates the prices. The costs vary but are arranged in a package format that includes accommodations, breakfast, a round of golf each day, and a dinner each evening. Participants travel on day one, play golf on days two, three, and four and either return after golf on the last day or stay over and drive back home on day five. These outings are not only for the golfers, but also include the wives. In most cases, if the women play golf, they are invited to play in the tournaments. If not, some other entertainment may be arranged in advance. The outings are limited to the number of rooms available or the number of players a golf course can accommodate in a single round. These limitations always insure that the available slots are quickly filled.

Leonard Green and I began another summer outing in the mid 1990s. This one is always in Santee, South Carolina, and we always reserve the first week in June for our outing. It's also for both men and women and is a three day event. The prices are so attractive that Jorge Buendia once proclaimed, "Hell, I can't even stay home for that kind of money!" We usually leave on Sunday around noon, drive to Santee, and arrive in plenty of time for a leisurely dinner on Sunday evening. The drive is all interstate and to ward off the boredom of the five hour trip, we always get a good audio book that we can listen to both going and coming back. One summer I selected *Toxin* by Robin Cook. He's one of my favorite authors and if you're not familiar with Robin Cook books, they are usually about some aspect of medicine. This one had to do with some mysterious poisons emanating from a slaughter house. There were very graphic descriptions of the slaughter and processing of meats, particularly beef. It was sheer entertainment for Jorge and me, but Bill Bynum took it so seriously that he swore off eating hamburger for many months after hearing the book. After Bill had such a bad reaction to *Toxin*, I selected other authors for subsequent trips. We heard *The Runaway Jury*, by John Grisham on one trip, and *The Brethren*, also by John Grisham on another. He is one author that we can all agree on.

Once we arrive at the motel in Santee, I stay pretty busy with the organization of the golf for three days in a row. I always take my laptop computer along with a small printer. I have all the players in a data base with the necessary information on each one, such as average points, pairing preferences, etc. We divide the players into four flights according to their average points. The top twenty-five percent are designated as A players, and the rest are designated as B, C, and D players according to their point averages. Pairings for each day's play are such that the players can make up their own playing foursome. However, the players in any given foursome will probably not be the players in the team that is put together for competition. We devised a system that absolutely eliminates sandbagging or picking a winning team. We do this by allowing the players to select the teams by blind draw after the round is played. At eight o'clock each evening, we meet in a large meeting room provided for us by the motel. At this meeting we have the A players draw their other three team members. They draw three numbers from a hat and I correlate the number drawn to a B, C, or D player, move each player to the A player's team together with the point scores that the player posted for the day's round. After all A players have completed the drawing, I tap a key on the computer keyboard and the data base spits out a report containing team members, points required and points scored. The report also reflects the calculation of points, plus or minus, produced when the team's point quota is subtracted from the team's actual points for the day. All we have to do then is announce the winning teams. This method of competing does a couple of things. First, it allows the players the freedom to play in the foursome of their choice. This is particularly important to some of the women. Second, it encourages the players in each foursome to abide by the rules and see to it that the other members of their foursome do likewise. Regardless of who they are playing with, they know that person will probably be their opponent in the team competition. We do whatever we can to insure that players abide by USGA rules with only one exception. We do allow golfers to improve their lie in the fairway of the hole they're playing. As stated earlier, senior golfers frequently violate the USGA rules of golf in several ways, such as improving their lie or forgetting to count all their strokes.

"Golf appeals to the idiot and the child in us. Just how childlike golfers become is proven by their frequent inability to count past five." –John Updike

The Santee outing is one of the most popular in which I participate. I believe it's because we do everything possible to make the competition fair, we keep the costs at bargain basement rates, and we emphasize enjoyment of the game over scoring or winning. We all love to win, but if we never win, we still enjoy the game and the fellowship of the group.

The latest trip to Santee occurred on June 6, 2004. We drove up on Sunday, played a tournament at Wyboo Plantation on Monday, June 7th, a second tournament at the Players Club at Wyboo on June 8th, and the third and last tournament at Santee National on June 9th. We had our biggest group ever at this outing. We began with eighty-four golfers but with any group that ranges in age between fifty-five and eighty-five there are usually some health problems that reduce our number. One of the ladies dropped out the first day because of a shoulder problem and on the second day one of the players had a death in his family and had to drop out. On the third day we lost another player because of back problems so we finished with eighty-one out of eighty-four players, which I think is pretty good. Since the winning scores are based on the combined number of points for each team, we simply had three three-man teams. This works out well and when a three-man team wins they get to split the winnings three ways instead of four.

Jorge Buendia and I drove up to Santee together and the audio book I chose this year was John Grisham's latest, *The Last Juror*. Although Bill Bynum now lives in North Alabama and had to travel over seven hours to get there, he and a mutual acquaintance of ours from our working days came to Santee to participate in our tournaments. We even paired our old foursome together for one round. Jorge, Bill, Tom, and I played the first tournament together. It was almost like old times, but we could all tell that age is taking its toll on all of us.

Every year after the Santee trip, I critique the tournament process we go through in an effort to make it smoother and less time consuming. This year we had a few minor problems, but for the most part it went very well. On Monday night we completed the drawings and announced the winners in about forty minutes, which I thought was pretty good. Dave Osborn came up with the suggestion to convene only the A players at 7:30 p.m., and complete the drawings. Then have all the participants present at 8:00 p.m. for the awards ceremony. We tried this on Tuesday, and it worked very well and with a lot less confusion. Had it not rained on us the last day with only two holes left to play, we would have had what is probably the most successful outing ever this year. Everyone seemed to enjoy the golf and fellowship, and we have already reserved the first week in June 2005 for the next trip. We are saddened only by the fact that two of our regulars are seriously ill and probably won't make it to Santee again.

l-r, Bill, Tom, Author, Jorge in Santee, SC

Chapter Thirteen

Friendly Bets

Our foursome always has a little bet going when we play together. We usually play a round robin. That's a team bet where two players play their best ball against the other two players. The partners change after each six holes, thereby insuring that each person is partners with every other member of the foursome during a round. We also sweeten the kitty for birdies, greenies, and sandies.

Everyone knows that a birdie is one under par, i.e. a two on a par three. A greenie is awarded to the person closest to the pin in one on a par three green. The ball must be on the green from the tee, and in order to collect the greenie the player must score a par. Sandies are similar to greenies in that a player scores a sandie if he gets out of a sand trap and into the hole with a score of par. The sand trap can be a fairway trap or a greenside trap. In the event that a player scores a rare eagle or hole-in-one, the bets for that hole are doubled. Another bet that is a lot of fun is the rabbit. When we start the round, the rabbit is running. The rabbit is caught when one player scores lower on a hole than anyone else. He keeps the rabbit only as long as no one beats him on a hole. If someone beats the player holding the rabbit, it turns the rabbit loose and he is running again and available for capture by any player. The player who holds the rabbit at the end of the front nine wins a rabbit from each of the other players. This is an individual bet as opposed to a team bet. A second rabbit is available on the back nine. The bets can be for whatever amount on which the players agree. Since the players in our foursome are high rollers, we play for quarters on everything but the rabbit. The rabbit is a dollar.

Over the years there has been very little change in the betting in our foursome. However, from time to time we have made modifications. Most of the changes have been discarded after a short time and the betting reverted to that described in the preceding paragraph. One such change occurred in a round we played at Pine Bluff Golf Club in Eastman, Georgia. We decided to modify the betting so that the winner of a hole was decided by the sum of the score of the two partners against the other two. For example, if player A has a par on a par four hole and his partner, player B has a six, their total is ten. Let's say their opponents, player C has par and his partner has a five for a total of 9. Player C and D would win because their total is less. Under the normal system, the two teams would tie because the better ball on each team was a four. We all played well in Eastman, but I had one of my better rounds. Each quarter won or lost is called a scat, and on that particular day Bill Bynum shot a 76 and lost 19 scats! Needless to say, that modification was dropped immediately after that round and has not been resurrected since. From time to time, Jorge suggests that we pay lap money for the person holding the rabbit. This would mean that the player holding the rabbit on each hole would collect an amount, probably a quarter, for each hole for which he held the rabbit, regardless of who wins the rabbit on hole-nine and eighteen. Perhaps we'll adopt this modification one day, but so far it's been rejected when the betting is agreed upon at the beginning of a round.

The betting arrangements were once blamed for a major flare up in our foursome. We were playing at one of our outings in Santee, South Carolina, and at the end of the round there was a violent disagreement between Tom Hartstern and Jorge Buendia. It was the last day of our trip, and we were leaving after the round to drive back home. Tom was driving alone, and Bill and I were riding with Jorge. Tom had accused Jorge of not paying a previous bet, and therefore he was not going to pay Jorge for that day's bets.

In retrospect it seems improbable that such a disagreement would arise from such a trivial thing. But this resulted in Jorge and Tom refusing to play golf with each other ever again. Bill and I talked to each one of them separately, and we could not get an agreement by them to settle their differences so that we could continue to play as a foursome. Jorge and Tom had ridden in the same golf cart with each other for years! Suddenly, they refused to even play in the same foursome, let alone ride with each other. After several weeks of playing the peace makers, Bill and I decided that we'd offer to split up and one of us would ride with Tom and the other would ride with Jorge. We finally got them to agree and while playing in a senior dogfight at Barrington Hall Golf Club in Macon, we resumed playing as a foursome. Jorge and Tom always made cutting remarks to each other in a critical way. I think the nerve endings finally got worn to the point that the flare up over the betting at Santee just blew the whole relationship out of the water. To this day, five years after that disagreement at Santee, Jorge and Tom will not ride in the same golf cart together. They will, however, play in the same foursome and will speak to each other in a more or less civil way, particularly when they are partners.

Chapter Fourteen

Mannerisms and Habits

Everyone has certain mannerisms that sometimes grate on the nerves of others. Our foursome proved no exception to this. Jorge has a habit of plumb bobbing. Not just his putts, but practically every shot he hits. I've had a number of people ask me why Jorge plumb-bobs on the tee. There can be no explanation. I just respond by saying that it's a habit. I really think he began doing it to rattle or irritate his opponents and now he does it purely out of habit. Bill Bynum was particularly distracted by Jorge's plumb bobbing. I used to tell him, "Just ignore it and don't let it bother you."

I mentioned earlier that Jorge always drives his car to the golf courses we play. His propensity for driving doesn't end when we get to the golf course. He always wants to drive the golf cart. His operation of a cart would make any marshal wince. Regardless of where his ball may lay, he thinks he has to drive the cart to within a couple of yards of the ball, even if it's in the woods! Having been a marshal for several years, I may be a little more sensitive to his cart operation than most people, but he consistently drives too close to the greens, too close to the tees, and frequently drives into the fairway on holes where signs clearly prohibit them, especially par threes. Since the falling out between Jorge and Tom, it has been my lot to ride in the cart with Jorge so I know whereof I speak. What sacrifices we make to keep peace in the foursome!

Tom's mannerisms are the subject of much comment also. He's a very deliberate player. That's a nice way of saying he's slow. I guess when he and Jorge were good friends and rode in the same cart together, Tom got accustomed to riding as a passenger in the cart. Now he never operates the cart. This frees him to go wandering off, usually in the direction of his ball. We have to warn him frequently about walking in front of someone who is about to hit. Sometimes he'll walk all the way across the fairway to his ball, look at his lie, then walk all the way back to the cart to select a club. He selects the club, walks back to his ball, but decides he has the wrong club. Now he must walk all the way back to the cart and make another selection. Is it any wonder he's slow? We've tried to get him to take a couple of clubs with him when he goes to his ball. After all, he's played these courses and shots so many times, he must have a good idea of the distances and should be able to judge what club or clubs he might need for the shot. Our protestations are met with a silent glare! Frequently, Tom is in his own world and just ignores those around him.

We all enjoy ribbing Tom. Several years ago, soon after he had become familiar with the Internet, he would often arrange to meet women over the net. They would send him pictures, and he would make arrangements to meet them. He contacted one who lived in Texas and one day he confided to us that he was going to drive to Texas to meet her. We thought it incredible that anyone would drive 1300 miles to see a person based on a few email messages. We gave him a hard time by asking, "How do you know this is really her picture?" or "How do you know she's really a woman?" "What if you get out there and she's married to a big burly jealous man?" Although he had no credible answers, he did drive to Texas to meet this woman, and when he came back he was beaming. About a month later, he drove to Texas again to see her. When he came back the second time, he announced that he was going to marry her. Then we began to question him about where they'd live, in Texas or in Georgia. We told him that if she ever laid eyes on that wilderness home of his, she would never come to Georgia. He'd just have to live in Texas and that would mess up our foursome! I don't know if our ribbing caused him to have second thoughts or not, but he made a third trip to Texas. However, when he came back the love affair was over. It seems the lady was seeing her boss romantically, and she was reluctant to end that relationship.

It wasn't long, however, until he had made contact with another woman. This one was in Florida and he made a big deal about the fact that she had a doctorate in psychology. After several weeks of communicating back and forth, she agreed to come to Georgia to meet Tom. He was to pick her up at the Airport in Atlanta, and she would spend several days with him at his home in the wilderness. When Tom told us of his plans, we were skeptical to say the least and had a few thousand negative words to say about the whole relationship. He could not be dissuaded, however, and made the final arrangements. We found out much later that the arrangements included the price of a round-trip airline ticket sent to her in the form of a money order. Of course, when she got the money, the trip was cancelled, and Tom was left holding the bag! She had done a psychological number on Tom. We ragged him so much about this incident that he clammed up and would not tell us about any subsequent arrangements he made with his Internet dates.

His other Internet adventures included the purchase of a 1987 Susuki 1800 touring motorcycle on eBay. It was similar to the one on which he much earlier had ridden from coast to coast. This time he won an auction bid for $1800 and then had to go to Idaho Falls, Idaho, to pick it up. He flew out to Idaho Falls, picked up the motorcycle, and spent another $300 to prepare it for riding back home. He said, "I just wanted to ride that big beautiful motor one more time." He said while crossing Kansas he passed eighteen wheelers doing eighty miles per hour. He once passed one and was hit by a crosswind on the plains and almost lost it in the median. He did make it back home in one piece and often rode the motorcycle to our golfing dates with his golf bag strapped to the luggage carrier and his golf shoes in the saddle bags. He kept the motorcycle for several months and finally decided he had experienced enough adventures. He gave the motorcycle to his doctor who thought it was the best of the touring motorcycles.

Tom's less adventurous interests are gardening and growing African violets. He once bragged to me about the tomatoes he grew in his garden. Bill Bynum was a gardener and grew some fine vegetables in his garden and would frequently give Jorge and me some of his bounty. We told Tom that if he really had too many tomatoes, he should bring his friends some of them. It wasn't long before Tom showed up at the golf course and handed me a brown paper bag. Inside were several tomatoes about the size of walnuts. I was so amused that I had a hard time containing my laughter. Were these the great tomatoes he'd grown in his garden? What was the name of these tomatoes? Were they cherry tomatoes? Did he actually cultivate these tomatoes, or did they just grow wild? We ribbed him so badly that he finally just puffed up like an old bull frog and pouted. Now, if I ask him about his tomato crop, he just says, "Go to hell!"

Chapter Fifteen

Special Moments

Have you ever wondered how some pros can recount every shot they hit in a particular tournament? I have, but there are moments in my golfing experience that I can remember like a motion picture film in my mind and some of those moments happened many years ago.

Tee Time Fidelity

When a foursome plays together over a long period of time, each member becomes aware of his obligation to show up for a golf date unless something absolutely catastrophic prevents it. This fidelity to the tee time was best demonstrated in our group recently by Tom Hartstern. While on his way to the golf course a deer darted out in front of him while he was traveling about fifty-five miles per hour in his 4 X 4 pickup. By reflex he swerved to miss the deer, hit a ditch, and when he tried to recover the pickup rolled several times. The pickup was totaled but fortunately Tom was unhurt. He managed to extricate himself from the wreckage just about the time a state trooper pulled up. The trooper just happened to be traveling on the same route a few miles behind Tom. The trooper, a young female, showed some concern for Tom's well being and tried to get him to go to the hospital for a checkup. "Can't do it," Tom said emphatically, "I have to go to the golf course."
"Are you serious?" asked the trooper. "You can suffer serious consequences from an accident without even knowing you're hurt!"
"Listen, little lady," Tom said, "if I don't show up for my tee time there will be more serious consequences!" Tom then convinced the trooper to drive him to the golf course. He got there for his tee time and played one of his better rounds in months.

Holes-in-one

I would guess that making a hole-in-one is a memory to keep forever. I've had two separated by over ten years. The first was on the number eight hole at River North Country Club, now called Healy Point. I was playing in a group that included Bill Bynum and Tom Hartstern, but I think Jorge Buendia was working that day. We played from the middle tees, and I hit a four iron on a high trajectory. I followed the ball in flight until it hit the ground and I lost it. Everyone else did too. It appeared to be right of the pin by several feet, maybe even on the edge of the green. When we arrived at the green I began looking for my ball in the right rough and in the sand traps on the right of the green. When I couldn't find it, my playing partners also began to look for it. When we'd looked about everywhere it could be, I walked by the hole and noticed the ball in the cup. We speculated that it hit something on the right side of the green and caromed into the hole. It brought to mind the old adage, "they don't count how, just how many." I had my first hole-in-one but was a little disappointed that I didn't see the ball go into the hole.

My second hole-in-one came in 2003 at Waterford Golf Club in Bonaire, Georgia. The seventeenth hole is about 135 yards over a lake with a couple of gaping sand traps in front of the green. The green is slightly elevated from the tee, but a player is able to see a ball hit the green if the hole is placed near the center where it was on this occasion. I hit a seven iron into a slight breeze and hit it pretty good on a high trajectory. I saw it hit the green, bounce one time, and disappear. I was playing in a group that included Tom, Jorge, and Dave Osborn. Bill had already moved back to Alabama. Dave told me it went in the hole, but there are a lot of ways a ball can disappear on that green so I didn't get excited until I got to the green and couldn't see a ball on the green. I walked to the hole and savored the moment as I took the ball out of the cup.

My brother, Charles, didn't start playing golf until after he was fifty years old and I think he's had six holes-in-one. On the other hand, Bill Bynum has played golf for over sixty years and has never had a hole-in-one.

"Man blames fate for other accidents, but feels personally responsible when he makes a hole-in-one." -Author Unknown

Frigid Fairways

Early in my golfing life, I learned to endure bad weather in order to complete a round of golf. I remember playing in San Antonio, Texas, in the winter time when we had to wait for the greens keepers to spray the greens with water to melt away the frost on the greens.

There are other moments associated with golf that I'll never forget. One Monday in February, we drove to Tifton, Georgia, to play golf at a course by the name of Sun Sweet Hills. It was a cold but sunny day and we drove all the way from Macon to Tifton on Interstate 75, a distance of about ninety miles. Jorge was driving the Oldsmobile diesel and the passengers were Bill Bynum, Bill Harrison, and me. The conversation during the trip was stimulating as usual, and we were completely oblivious to the outside temperature. It actually looked warm out there, and it's not all that unusual to have nice weather in February in the Middle Georgia area. We arrived at Sun Sweet Hills and were ready to get out and play some golf. I opened the right front door and the frigid temperature and brisk wind almost took my breath away. If you've ever jumped into a pool when the water was very cold you can imagine the sensation. We quickly bundled up in our winter togs which consisted of coats, gloves, and wool caps that came down over our ears. When we began to play, the wind was blowing about twenty miles-per-hour and felt like it would cut right through you like a Samurai's sword. I even got out my rain suit and put it on over my other clothes. We finished the round, but the only thing I remember about that course is that I was never more miserable during a round of golf. If all my golf had to be played in that kind of weather, I'd quit and never miss it. Sun Sweet Hills is probably a nice course and certainly not responsible for the weather, but it conjures up such bad memories we've never been back.

One other round I remember for a very similar reason. Bill Bynum and I drove to Jackson, Georgia, every month on the second Tuesday to play in a senior scramble. Hickory Hills Golf Club keeps a 3 X 5 card on all the seniors who play in the monthly scrambles with the number of points we normally pull. The players are categorized as A, B, C, and D players according to their point quotas. Then each team competes against the other teams. The total number of participants is usually around 120 and we began play from a shot-gun start at 10:00 a.m. The entry fee was fifteen dollars and included lunch. Bill and I played in the tournament on the second Tuesday in December. After the tournament, the owner announced that he was having a Christmas tournament the following week and would be giving some really good prizes along with a meal of turkey and dressing with all the trimmings instead of the normal fare of fried chicken. The price would be the same as the normal scramble. We decided it was too good a deal to pass up, so we went back the next week to play in the Christmas tournament. We were a little late teeing off because the putting green was covered with ice, and they figured the greens would be about the same. That would have been deterrent enough for most people but not us. We went ahead with our game and almost froze to death. The winners of these scrambles usually ranged somewhere between eight and twelve under par and since each of the four players hit from the best of the four previous shots, all teams were normally under par by several shots. Our team at the Christmas tournament finished even par and never scored a single birdie. We were so cold that we were just grateful it was over. This was the second most miserable round of golf I can remember playing, the most miserable being Sun Sweet Hills.

Water Hazards

We played at Randolph Air Force Base once when it was raining lightly, just enough to get the equipment wet, but not hard enough for us to quit. Cotton and I were playing with Gene Herzog, who worked with us. Gene was a fairly proficient golfer, but he had a tendency to throw his club when he hit a bad shot. We were walking and pulling our clubs on a pull-cart, so it wasn't unusual for us to walk directly to our ball and prepare to hit while another golfer was hitting. We were careful not to walk in the line of play of the other golfers, but sometimes we'd be left or right of their line nearer the green. I had approached my ball and selected a club when I heard the pulsating swoosh, swoosh, swoosh of a golf club spinning through the air near me. Gene had thrown his club with a mighty heave and it had come dangerously close to hitting me. I very calmly picked up his club, walked to where Gene was standing, and said to him, "Gene, if you ever hit me with a club, I'll wrap it around your head!" Lucky for me he never hit me, and I didn't have to keep that promise. On another occasion we were playing the eleventh, a par three of 183 yards with a lake just left of a narrow fairway that ran all the way from the tee to the green. It was necessary to hit over the lake or draw the ball slightly to reach the green. Gene took a mighty swing and hooked his ball into the lake. He walked to his bag and jammed the club hard into the bag. He then picked up the bag, including the pull-cart, walked to the front of the tee, and heaved the bag, cart, and all into the lake. That ended his round for the day, since he had to wade into the lake to retrieve his equipment, take it back to the club house, and clean it up for the next time.

"If you are going to throw a club, it is important to throw it ahead of you, down the fairway, so you don't have to waste energy going back to pick it up." - Tommy Bolt

The Homestead

In April of 1987, I attended a five day seminar for executives and account managers at IBM's facility in San Jose, California. IBM provided accommodations for its guests on the plant grounds. The compound was dubbed "The Homestead." It included motel-like rooms, a dining facility where all meals were provided, a swimming pool, and a nine-hole golf course. My IBM account manager, John Barrow, and I flew out together, and he had advised me to take my golf clubs, which I did. During the week that I was there, we had a couple of afternoons off to visit the sights in the area. In addition to playing the nine-hole course at the homestead in the afternoons after our business sessions were finished, John suggested that we might be able to get a tee time at Pebble Beach. He had someone in the office call but there were no tee times available at Pebble during the times we could play. They did tell us that we could play Spyglass Hill as an alternative. We agreed and on a Thursday afternoon we drove to Carmel and then to Spyglass Hill for an unforgettable round of golf. John and I were paired with a vacationing couple from southern California. I took my camera along and have the round pretty well documented. The scenery on the course was spectacular, and the course played very difficult with its unforgiving rough and oceanside greens. The most outstanding memory I have of the rough was something called Ice Plants. They are thick and look almost like cacti without the stickers. When your ball comes to rest in them it's impossible to hit it out. You just have to take an unplayable lie penalty and go from there. The cost of playing Spyglass was not cheap. We paid ninety dollars for an eighteen-hole round, but I figured it was the only time I'd have a chance to play a storied layout like Spyglass Hill, so I paid the fee and enjoyed the round. After we finished playing golf, we rode over to Pebble Beach, parked in the parking lot, visited the club house and walked the seventeenth and eighteenth holes. We then took the "17 mile drive" down the coast and enjoyed the sunset on the Pacific Ocean. It was a great experience, but I couldn't afford to do it very often.

Author at #4 Spyglass Hill

Author at Pebble Beach

The Reunion

I was instrumental in organizing and promoting a fiftieth anniversary reunion of my 1953 high school graduating class. My involvement began in a telephone conversation with one of my old high school buddies, Thurman Carver. During a phone conversation sometime in 2000 we observed that our graduating class had only two reunions, the tenth and the twenty fifth. We thought it would be appropriate to have a fiftieth. That's all I needed to start the ball rolling. I began to build a data base of our classmates' addresses and phone numbers. I solicited help from the classmates I contacted and with all the help I could get, it still took over two years to locate the surviving class members. I even built a web site and posted the names of all those contacted, those deceased and the latest news regarding the reunion.

One of the activities we planned was a golf tournament for those who wanted to participate, and several did. Given the popularity of golf, I was somewhat surprised that more of the classmates did not choose to participate. We had only two foursomes, but it was a pleasure to golf with some of the people I'd not seen in fifty years.

Charles Rainwater was chosen as the chairman of our planning committee and since I attended all the committee meetings, we always planned a round of golf during my visits to the Albertville, Alabama, area. Charles is one of those people who never played golf with any regularity until he retired. He was sixty years of age before he began playing. When I located him, he had just recently returned to Albertville after retiring from the Gold Kist Poultry Company. He first played when he was the division accounting manager in Russellville, Alabama. He's never had an official handicap but did have a personal best round of 75. He currently shoots in the mid to high 80s and works at it as hard as anyone I know. He's a member of the Albertville Country Club and plays five days per week, Monday through Friday. His favorite professional is Tom Watson, and his most unforgettable golfing experience was playing in the 1997 McDonald's Ladies Pro Am practice round in Wilmington, Delaware.

Charles is one of only two guys who married members of our graduating class, and he and his wife, Betty, have already celebrated their fiftieth wedding anniversary. He served in the Army from 1954 to 1956 as a mechanic, attended Snead State College and Jacksonville State College but never graduated. Golf was not a pastime he pursued during those days.

The Masters

During the first few years I lived in Macon, we went to the Masters several times to see the practice rounds. That was during the time when you could just walk up to the gate and purchase a daily ticket. Now of course, you must have pre-purchased tickets to view practice rounds. In order to obtain tickets you must get on a waiting list, and that waiting list is very long. It's been almost impossible to get tickets to the tournament for many years, but one year Bill Bynum's neighbor let us use his to attend the first round on Thursday. Personally, I enjoyed attending the practice rounds more than I did the actual tournament. Access to the course and to the players, was much better at the practice rounds. You could also use your camera and take snapshots of the course and the players. Cameras are frowned upon during tournament play.

The players seem to be friendlier at the practice rounds and tend to have a little fun. One year we watched Lee Trevino as he played his practice round. A pro playing behind him hit a ball within a few yards of him. He just walked over and hit the ball back to the player. On another occasion, when a ball came a little too close to him, he nonchalantly walked over, picked the ball up, and tossed it into a lake.

On another occasion, we were watching Billy Casper practice at the sixteenth tee and he gave us a demonstration on how to get over the water. He used a four or five iron from the tee and somehow made the ball bounce on the water three or four times before it hopped out on the other side barely on the green.

The Masters is like no other golfing event I've ever attended. To walk the grounds of the Masters at Augusta is like walking through a cathedral. You feel like you must whisper and walk carefully over the grounds that are so immaculately manicured that it seems not a blade of grass is out of place. The flowering shrubs are magnificent in their beauty and arrangement around the course and the tall pines are majestic. Literally hundreds of care-takers roam the course and attend to the least of details. If you drop a candy wrapper, a cigarette butt, a bottle cap, or tab from a soda pop can, it is immediately picked up and disposed of by the staff. Refreshment stands sell sandwiches, soda pop, and coffee at very reasonable prices, and they are all served with green napkins. The caddies are equipped with small containers of green sand, fertilizer, and grass seeds with which to repair divots.

There is more attention given to detail than you'd expect in a large hospital's operating theater. As far as the golf is concerned, I personally think you see more on television than you do in person at the tournament, but the atmosphere isn't the same. Anyone who loves golf should enjoy the experience of walking the grounds at Augusta at least once during his life.

I made the trip to Augusta once more, and possibly for the last time, on April 6, 2004 for the practice round. A golfing friend, John Herren, came into the possession of four tickets. He and his lady friend used two of them and he offered the other two to Dave Osborn, another of our frequent golfing companions. Dave's wife couldn't attend because of a business commitment, so Dave called and asked if I'd like to go. We left at 6:30 a.m. and arrived at Augusta National at 9:30 a.m. We entered through the back gate that led to the area around the thirteenth, fifteenth, and sixteenth greens. After orienting ourselves, we decided to walk over to the ninth green and watch some of the pros tee off at number ten. The crowds were so massive that we had a hard time getting to the 10th tee, so we walked to the general area of the twelfth in hopes of watching the tee shots from there. Once again the crowds made it impossible to see any action from the ground and the bleacher seats were full. We then walked back to where we started and finally found a seat in the bleachers overlooking the thirteenth green. We watched a number of players approach thirteen, putt out and tee off on fourteen. After about an hour we moved to the bleachers overlooking the fifteenth green and watched the approach shots and putting there. From this same vantage point we could see the sixteenth green but not the tee. A number of players were skimming shots over the lake and onto the green as I'd seen Billy Casper do many years earlier. It was a crowd pleaser and we could tell by the sound of the crowds whether a player made the green or came up short in the water. We spent about two hours here before deciding to leave around 2:00 p.m. I enjoyed seeing the course once again, but was sorely disappointed with our inability to gain good vantage points to see the action. I wanted to see my favorite pro, Arnold Palmer, playing for the fiftieth consecutive time in the Masters, but he teed off at about 1:00 p.m. and we needed to leave before he could have gotten to our vantage point.

I still love watching the Masters on television each year, and I got a little teary eyed watching Arnold Palmer play his final round on April 9, 2004. I noticed that he still uses band aids on his fingers, as he had done at Randolph AFB in 1961. I don't know if anyone else noticed, but I saw the band aids on each finger of his ungloved hand.

When you stop to think about it, it's amazing that he has played in fifty consecutive Masters Tournaments. He had already played in his first Masters when I first played golf forty nine years ago. Time really does fly when you're having fun!

Chapter Sixteen

Starting a Senior Golfers Association

Assuming that you'd like to start a senior golfers' association in your area, I'll tell you how I'd go about it.

First make a list of all those you know in the fifty-five and up age group who enjoy playing golf. Get as much information as possible on each of them, such as name, address, telephone number, and handicap if they have one. Start contacting them and seeing if they are interested in forming an association of golfers, who would like to play once each month on a particular weekday. When you find individuals who agree with the concept, ask them to contact anyone they know who would like to become a member. You'll be surprised how fast the number grows. You might even create an application form that prospective members can complete. At the end of this chapter I'll include a sample application that you can use as a pattern. If you have a personal computer, start building a data base of all the information you collect. One of the most popular software packages available is Microsoft Works. It contains software for the data base, as well as a word processor and spread sheet and will be all you need to prepare membership lists, mailing labels, newsletters, and pairing sheets.

The next thing you'll need is a data base of all the golf courses in your geographic area. In this data base you'll need the name, address, telephone number, name of the head golf professional, manager, or owner. You might also keep notes on the directions to each course so that you can give driving directions to the people who will play in the group. Keep this information available so that when you get enough people who want to participate, you can negotiate the price for a tournament with the number of players that want to participate. A sample data collection form is provided at the end of this chapter.

As you collect the data described above, you might want to get your own foursome together and visit each course. If the course is private, don't let that stop you from talking to the person in charge about your group playing there. Be sure to emphasize that you are a non-profit senior golf association. Many private courses will welcome large groups on a weekday when no other special activities are scheduled.

When you have signed up a significant number of golfers, you might want to think about a name for the group, such as the XYZ Senior Golf Association. Eventually, you'll need to draw up some bylaws to formalize the organization and to specify how it will be operated and governed. Following this chapter, I'll include a sample set of bylaws that can be used and modified to fit your particular group.

During the organizational phase, you'll need to consider how to finance your activities. Some groups are financed by annual membership dues and a fixed entry fee for each tournament. This is the most straight forward method and it gives the governing body the parameters it will need to negotiate with the courses that will be played. An alternative could be a nominal fee for annual dues to cover administrative costs, some amount for the prize pool, and the actual amount charged by the particular golf course for each specific tournament.

A policy statement distributed annually to each individual member is a good idea so that everyone knows what to expect from the organization. A sample policy statement is provided at the end of this chapter.

A newsletter should be prepared and issued each month on a regular schedule. This is the primary method of communicating with the membership. Normally, it consists of any announcements that need to be disseminated, the results of the most recently completed tournament, and an announcement regarding the next tournament to be played. This can usually be accomplished on one printed page which can be copied in sufficient numbers to distribute to all members. A sample is provided at the end of this chapter.

Other questions will no doubt arise. If you get stuck and need other suggestions, I'll try to help if you'll go to my web site at:

http://members.cox.net/jbowl35a

This is the end of my adventure in golf—so far. I wish for each of you as much joy as I've received from the game and from the friends I've made as a result of it. Happy Golfing!

SAMPLE

MEMBERSHIP APPLICATION
XYZ Senior Golf Association
P.O. Box 1234
Anywhere, USA

Name:_____

Mailing
Address:_____

City:_____ State:_____ ZIP:_____

Birthdate:_____ Spouse's Name:_____

Telephone Numbers:_____
                           Home   Bus.   Mobile

I am a member of_____ Golf/Country Club

Handicap:____ or Average Score for 18 holes:_____

Sponsors:_____

SAMPLE

Golf Course Data

XYZ Senior Golf Association
P.O. Box 1234
Anywhere, USA

Course Name: _____

Address: _____

City: _____ State: _____ ZIP: _____

Telephone Numbers: _____

Primary Contact: _____ Title: _____

Private: _____ Semi-Private: _____ Public: _____

Advertised Fee (if available): _____

RULES AND BYLAWS
XYZ SENIOR GOLF ASSOCIATION

ARTICLE I – NAME

The name of the Association will be "XYZ Senior Golfers Association".

ARTICLE II – PURPOSE

The purpose of this association shall be to promote fellowship and friendly competition in golf among Anywhere Senior Golfers.

ARTICLE III – MEMBERSHIP

Section A – Eligibility:

Any male resident of the Anywhere area who is 55 years of age or older, holding amateur status, may be recommended by two (2) members in good standing. The application must be approved by a majority vote of the Board of Directors.

Section B – Number of Members:

The number of active members shall be limited to 150.

Section C – Classes of Membership:

1. A Full Regular Membership is a member whose dues are current and who has reached his 55th birthday.
2. Members who cannot participate in more than six tournaments in any one year because of sickness may be placed on inactive status and

restored to full membership when they are again able to play golf. Members who wish to be placed on inactive status must request it and must pay annual dues at the designated times.

Section D – Termination of Membership:

1. If a member has not paid his annual dues within thirty (30) days after May 1st each year, he will be delinquent and his membership will automatically be terminated.
2. If any member's actions or conduct are cause for complaint and these charges are brought before the Board of Directors, his membership may be terminated after he is given the opportunity for a hearing by the Board. The Board's decision will be final and he will be notified of the Board's action by the Secretary/Treasurer.

Section E – Membership Year:

The membership year will begin on May 1st and end on April 30th of the following year.

ARTICLE IV – BOARD OF DIRECTORS

Section A – Composition of the Board:

The Board of Directors shall consist of six (6) members – the President, Vice-President, Secretary/Treasurer, and three (3) Board Members. All Officers and Board Members will be elected annually by the membership for a term of one year. The President will designate a nominating committee each year at the March tournament. The nominating committee will present their nominations at the April tournament. Once the nominating committee report is presented, nominations may be accepted from the floor. Elections will be completed at the April tournament and the new officers will take office on May 1st.

Section B – Duties and Responsibilities:

The Board of Directors shall interpret and apply all matters relative to the bylaws. They shall establish overall policy of the Association. They shall fill all vacancies which may occur in the membership or on the Board between annual elections. They shall hear any complaints and be the final arbiter of such matters. They may employ such outside assistance as necessary to accomplish the stated goals of promoting and producing monthly golf tournaments.

Section C – Voting Procedure:

Meetings of the Board shall be called by the President. However, any three (3) members of the Board may call special meetings upon notification in writing to all Board members. A quorum of the Board shall consist of any four (4) members and a quorum must be present to conduct any business of the Association.

ARTICLE V – ADMINISTRATIVE OFFICERS

Section A – President:

The President shall serve as presiding officer at all meetings of the membership and the Board of Directors. He shall execute signature cards at all banks which hold Association funds to authorize expenditure of funds in these accounts. He shall appoint committees as they become necessary. He shall serve as Chairman of the Tournament Committee and be directly responsible for securing tournament sites, meals and other necessities required for monthly membership golf tournaments.

Section B – Vice-President:

    The Vice-President shall serve as President in all of the capacities outlined above in the event of the President's temporary inability to serve. The Vice-President will automatically assume the Presidency if that office is permanently vacated for any reason.

Section C – Secretary/Treasurer:

    The Secretary/Treasurer shall be responsible for receipt and distribution of all funds of the Association. He shall execute signature cards, and is authorized to draw checks against these funds for Association expenditures. He shall maintain accurate records of all receipts and expenditures and shall submit a financial report at each meeting to the Board. He will keep minutes of the Board meetings to go into the permanent record of the Association.

ARTICLE VI – REVENUES

Section A – Sources:

1. Each member shall be charged annual dues in an amount to be determined by the Board of Directors.

Section B – Disbursements:

1. The Secretary/Treasurer shall pay all bills incidental to the production and mailing of the monthly newsletter plus any special mailing which may be necessary. He shall make all refunds of any dues which may be in order.
2. All expenses incurred in the conduct of the monthly tournaments will be paid by the Secretary/Treasurer. These will include charges

by the Host Clubs, food costs, prizes and gratuities.

ARTICLE VII RECORDS

Section A – Roster:
The Secretary shall maintain a current roster of all members of the Association. This roster shall reflect all pertinent information on each member as to age, address, telephone number, etc. There will also be kept a list of eligible applicants showing date of application.

Section B – Minutes:
The Secretary/Treasurer shall maintain a complete written record of the minutes of all Board and membership meetings. These minutes shall accurately reflect all actions taken by the Board relating to Association business. These minutes will be kept in a permanent record which will be turned over to succeeding administrations each year.

Section C – Financial Records:
The Secretary/Treasurer shall maintain complete and accurate records of all funds on hand or on deposit, which belong to the Association. He shall render a coherent statement on these accounts to the Board at each meeting.

ARTICLE VIII – BOARD MEETINGS

The President shall convene a meeting of the Board of Directors no less than once each calendar quarter for the purpose of reviewing the progress of the Association. The meeting will examine the following matters:
1. Membership changes and applications.
2. Complaints and suggestions, if any.
3. Minutes of the previous meeting.

4. Treasurer's report and balance sheets.

ARTICLE IX

The bylaws of this Association and amendments thereto will be ratified by the membership.

These bylaws were ratified by the membership on _____

(date)
Attested by:
_____
(Secretary/Treasurer)

These bylaws were amended by the membership on _____

Attested by: _____

(Secretary/Treasurer)

SAMPLE

Board of Directors Policy Statement

1. Golf tournaments are scheduled every (number) (day) of each month.

2. A newsletter is mailed to each member, usually the (number) week of the month, announcing the results of the last tournament and furnishing information about the next tournament, i.e., location, date and time, cost, and the number that can play. Entry fees must be received not later than the (day) before the tournament on (day). Cancellations will be honored if called in by noon on the day before the tournament.

3. Scoring is via the point system, i.e., one for bogey, two for par, four for birdie and eight for eagle. Competition is divided into three flights. Each flight is composed of approximately one third of the golfers playing. There are ten winners in each flight. A prize is also given to the individual closest to the pin on the par three holes. A special gift will be awarded to any member scoring a hole-in-one during a regularly scheduled tournament.

4. Winners receive gift certificates that can be redeemed for merchandise at participating pro shops. Certificates may also be used towards the entry fee for a future tournament. <u>Certificates are void after 90 days.</u>

5. When no points can be scored, i.e., you lay bogey, please score a double bogey, pick up your

ball and go to the next hole. This helps speed up play.

6. You may lift, clean and place your ball, within one club-length, no nearer the hole, in the fairway of the hole you're playing. However, if you move your ball in the rough, add a penalty stroke.

7. Play is from the Senior Tees if available. If there are no Senior Tees, use the white tees.

8. Point quotas are adjusted after each tournament as follows:
    a. If you win, your points go up two.
    b. If you are minus three or more points, your points go down one.
    c. If you are minus one or two, or if you are plus and don't win, yours points will stay the same.

9. You may deduct $5.00 from the tournament fee if the tournament is played during the month of your birth. Happy birthday, but <u>NO</u> <u>CARRYOVERS!!</u>

10. Annual membership fees are due (month) 1st each year and are delinquent after (month) 31st. Membership will be terminated when dues are delinquent.

11. Membership may be terminated if you participate in less than five tournaments in a year. However, you may request inactive status in the event of serious illness.

12. Officers and Board Members are elected each year at the April tournament and take office on May 1st.

13. Guests may play in a scheduled tournament when sponsored by a member, provided a space is available and the guest pays the normal entry fee. Guests, however, will not be eligible for gift certificates.

SAMPLE

NEWSLETTER
(month) (year)

Membership Dues:
The (membership year) membership dues are payable and will be delinquent after (date).
The Board of Directors set membership dues at (amount) for this renewal.

Cell Phones:
We have had some complaints about cell phone use during the monthly tournaments. Please refrain from using cell phones on the course. You may have your contacts phone the pro shop to contact you in case of an emergency.

ELECTIONS:
The following Officers and Board Members were elected at Anywhere on (date):
President – John Doe; Vice-President – John Two; Secretary/Treasurer – John Three;
Members of the Board: Bill One, Bill Two and Bill Three.
Newly elected Officers and Board Members will take office effective (date).

Winners at Any Place Golf Club

0 – 17	18 – 22	23 & Up

Closest to the Pin:

JOHN D. BOWLING

Next Tournament:
WHERE: Some Place Golf Club, Anywhere, USA

WHEN: (date) (9:30 Shotgun Start)

COST: (amount) (deduct (amount) if your birthday is in(month)

Club phone number is (AC) Phone

LUNCH: On your own.
SOFT SPIKES: Required.

CUTOFF: We can take up to 112 entrants for this tournament. Waiting list will be determined by postmark date.